THE CAÑON FROM GRAND VIEW

Burton Holmes Traveloques

With Illustrations from Photographs By the Author

~ VOLUME SIX ~

The McClure Company
New York
MCMX

THE YELLOWSTONE NATIONAL PARK

The Yellowstone National Park

THE YELLOWSTONE region—that semi-mythical wonderland of yesterday—has become a fascinating reality
to the traveler of to-day.

Late in the sixties the attention of the world was directed to
an unexplored region in the northwestern corner of Wyoming.

Strange rumors had been set afloat concerning the existence there among the Rockies, near the head-waters of a
river called the Yellowstone, of an almost inaccessible
plateau, where mysterious phenomena of a most startling
character were grouped as in an enchanted amphitheater.

Accordingly a number of exploring-parties were sent out to confirm or to disprove the extravagant statements that had long been rife. When the leaders of these expeditions, on their return to civilization, submitted their reports, these were at first received incredulously; the world would not believe that wonders such as they described existed elsewhere than in the imagination of the daring travelers. But as the witnesses increased in number doubt gave place to belief, and the world awoke to the importance of their revelations. It was soon proved that a new Wonderland had been discovered; and Congress, acting with commendable promptitude, decreed that this territory where Nature had assembled so many of her marvelous creations, this land she had so long shrouded in mystery, should be set apart as a perpetual playground for the Nation.

Ask any traveler who has visited the Yellowstone National Park to describe it and he will reply, "It is indescribable."

My task is therefore not an easy one, since it is to describe the indescribable. Returning in August, from Greece to the United States, I was dreading the long mid-summer railway-ride over fully two thirds of our broad continent. "But," said a friend, "why

THE "NORTHLAND" AT BUFFALO

MACKINAC

do you go by rail?   Why don't you travel west by water?''
The thought was new to me, and I at once resolved to
take advantage of that splendid water-way which leads from
the Empire State to the Gates of the Great Northwest.

Accordingly the
porter is given in-
structions to ''put
us off at Buffalo,''
where we begin
our long voyage
around America's
vast inland seas.
Well worthy the
name of seas are
the waters trav-
ersed by the great
snow-white levia-
than, the ''North-
land.'' From

ON THE BRIDGE

New York State to Minnesota the traveler may speed in a
luxurious steamer, almost at railway pace.

Of the most delightful voyage through Erie, Huron, and
Superior I shall say little ; exhilarating as are the fresh lake
winds, and lovely as is the expanse of water over which we
speed, the winds and waters do not lend themselves to illus-
tration ; but among the few events that call for pictorial
record is the arrival at the gay summer port of Mackinac,
reached on the second morning.   The summer colony turns
out in force to welcome us.   Newspapers which are brought
on board tell us that throughout the length and breadth of
the land people are dying from the effects of the intense
August heat.   With selfish pleasure we recall two days of

AT THE MACKINAC PIER

IN THE "SOO" LOCKS

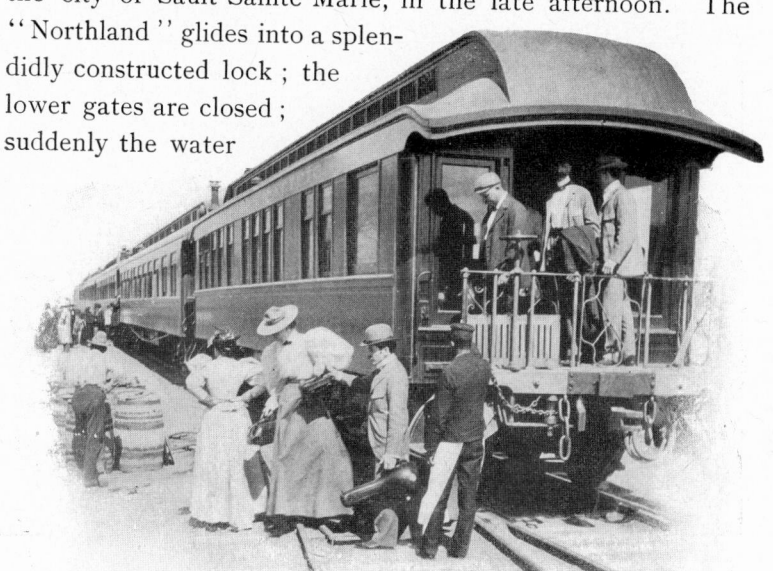

EN ROUTE

fresh, cool breezes, and thank our stars that we have wisely chosen to travel west by the water route.

On the pier we find a happy crowd of people whose only object in life is to keep cool and to enjoy themselves. Many of our fellow-passengers leave the ship at Mackinac, but their places are taken by others who embark for an excursion to the famous "Soo," the gateway to Lake Superior. We reach the "Soo," or, properly, the city of Sault Sainte Marie, in the late afternoon. The "Northland" glides into a splendidly constructed lock; the lower gates are closed; suddenly the water

ARRIVAL AT CINNABAR

COACHES FOR MAMMOTH HOT SPRINGS

at the upper end begins to act as if a geyser were striving to break forth, and slowly, steadily, lightly, as if instead of solid steel she were made but of snowy paper, the "Northland" rises eighteen feet, then pauses a moment before steaming northward upon the bosom of Superior to whose level she has been lifted so quietly and without appreciable delay.

THE CINNABAR STATION

We now enjoy a night and a day on the clear, deep waters of our greatest lake, and finally, three days after our departure from Buffalo, we reach Duluth. Thence by rail we hasten to the "Twin Cities," arriving just in time to join the friends with whom we are to travel to the Yellowstone.

Westward we are then whirled over the line of the Northern Pacific Railway, across Dakota and Montana, through the Bad Lands, along the lower course of the Yellowstone River to the little town of Cinnabar, on the border of the park, beyond which Uncle Sam will not permit the iron horse to pass. There are, however, other horses, and excellent ones, too, awaiting us ; a four-in-hand coach has been provided for our party, and in it we are soon installed with bags and cameras, umbrellas, linen-dusters, and a wealth of expectation. We give the signal for our departure ; a crack of the whip, a forward spring of the four horses, and we receive the first impression of a visit to the Yellowstone. It is this : In the foreground the backs of four tugging horses, on either side a mass of scrubby pines, before us a dusty road, and overhead a deep bright sky.

GARDINER CITY

FROM THE BOX-SEAT

Pictures like this fill the eye for many hours every day, but even this monotony itself is delightful. We drink in health at every breath. As we ride along through this bracing atmosphere, we are in love with life.

IN GARDINER CAÑON

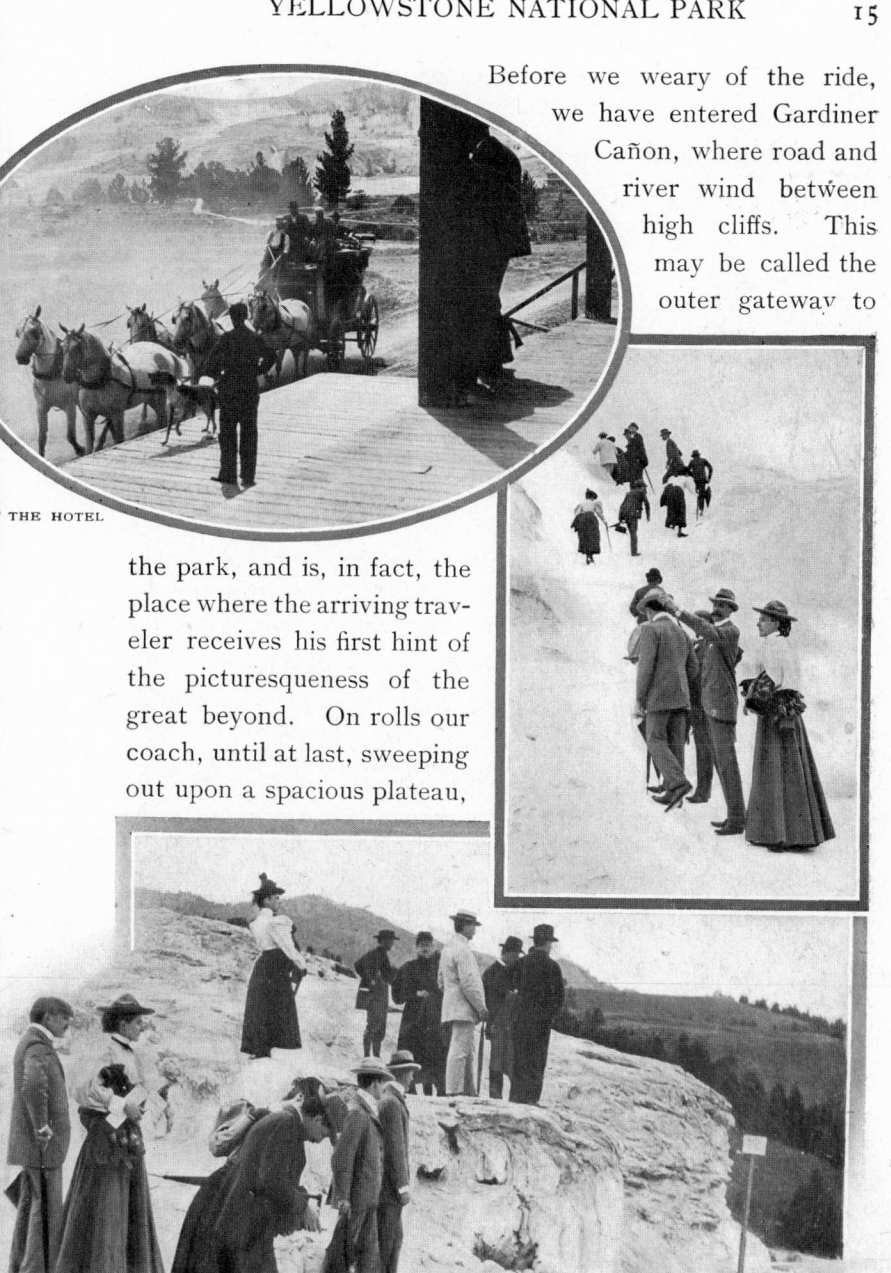

Before we weary of the ride, we have entered Gardiner Cañon, where road and river wind between high cliffs. This may be called the outer gateway to

THE HOTEL

the park, and is, in fact, the place where the arriving traveler receives his first hint of the picturesqueness of the great beyond. On rolls our coach, until at last, sweeping out upon a spacious plateau,

ON THE " FORMATION "

we are whirled rapidly up to the landing-stage of the Mammoth Hot Springs Hotel.

This hotel is one of a series of five big caravansaries recently established in the park. Not only at the springs, but at the two Geyser Basins, at the lake, and at the cañon the visitor will find excellent hotel accommodations, and he need fear no hardships in this much-traveled wilderness.

From the wide veranda we may see the terraces of the Mammoth Hot Springs, which are the first phenomena presented to the tourists' eyes. Let us at once respond to the attraction of yonder magnet, and hasten up the snow-white flank of the formation.

A MILLINERY MARVEL

"WE OURSELVES"

MAMMOTH HOT SPRINGS

Photograph by F. Jay Haynes, St. Paul

Formation of what, you ask? And the answer is, "Formation of formation"; for the name "formation" is applied not only to the wonderful terraced hill built up by action of the springs, but also to the material or deposit of which it is composed. "Formation" is a word that in time comes trippingly upon the tourist's tongue. "But what is formation?" we ask the voluble guide, who every day leads scores of visitors across it, and from many points of vantage indicates and describes the thousand and one phenomena that here surprise, delight, and mystify. Formation is simply the calcareous material deposited by the overflowing springs whose waters hold in solution carbonate of lime.

ORANGE GEYSER

Two hundred acres of formation have been thus created. From the valley floor rise terraces on terraces, some of them concealed among the pines far up the mountain-side. Three hours scarcely suffice for a mere visit to the wonders,

Photograph by F. Jay Haynes, St. Paul

MOUND TERRACE

grouped at many levels; as many days would not afford an opportunity for a detailed examination of them; as many weeks spent in contemplation of them would not enable the spectator to describe them. They are indescribable.

We first make our way over an expanse of snow-white formation. These colorless terraces may be said to be covered with the powdered bones of dead and vanished springs; where the waters have ceased to flow, all beauty and all color disappear. The first touch of color greets us at the terrace called the "Narrow Gauge." Along its crest a number of miniature geysers have raised their little cones. Most of them are content merely to boil and simmer, but their laziness is put to shame by one energetic little spout,

a tiny eruptive spring known as the Baby Geyser. It throws
a mighty liquid column, as fat as a pencil, to the astounding
height of seven inches. The waters of these springs flowing
unceasingly, down the slope, simultaneously build up and
tint the ridge. These waters are, however, only apprentices
in terrace-building and beginners in the art of terrace-tinting.
They are but neophytes, meekly practicing simple exercises
through which, in time, they will gain the skill required
to construct and color palaces like that of the Orange
Geyser, who is a master builder. On a foundation solid in
form and strong in color rests a superstructure of exquisite
daintiness, its overhanging balconies adorned with richly
tinted stalactites, each one of which is shedding liquid pearls.

Photograph by F. Jay Haynes, St. Paul

PULPIT TERRACE

But, though we are in midsummer, the trees all round about,
as if they realized the hopelessness of an attempt to rival this
unearthly beauty, put forth no leaves to cover their gaunt
nakedness. Beautiful as is this specimen of the waters'

workmanship, it is comparatively insignificant ; this is but a single isolated terrace — it is as nothing when we stand below the veritable mountain where the same phenomena are reproduced in countless numbers.   But here the fact is vividly impressed upon us that these springs, like mortal men, are subject to the awful law of death — the streams of life are ever changing in their course.   To-day they are flowing here from terrace to terrace, bowl to bowl, clothing them all with brilliancy and warmth, creating things of beauty to delight a generation.   They will in time forsake this slope, and then it, like the one down which the warm flood coursed in earlier days, will gradually grow white with age, dry with neglect, and finally, enfeebled by the alternating shocks of heat and cold, wind and rain, its graceful, snow-white, death-like forms will crumble to powder to be trampled underfoot by the travelers of future years.   But meantime other beautiful structures will have been created.   As we turn our

Photograph by F. Jay Haynes, St. Paul
CLEOPATRA TERRACE

dazzled eyes upon these marvelous productions of an unseen worker, we realize that perennial beauty is destined to reign here, as in the human race, although an impartial providence has decreed that individual loveliness shall be ephemeral.

Photograph by F. Jay Haynes, St. Paul

FORT YELLOWSTONE

These things attract and charm us just as flowers do— because of their freshness and their perishability.   Were this Pulpit of the Gods hewn in solid rock, were its colors applied in some indestructible lacquer, were we assured that in a thousand years it would not change or fade — why, half its charm would vanish.   Just as dewdrops on flowers add to their freshness and their charm, so are these forms made lovelier by the waters which clothe with life every pillar of the colonnade, every curve of the whole structure.   A thin veil of water, hot and clear, courses in quick pulsations over the beaded rims and down these tinted pillars until the terrace seems to live.   The glorious effect produced by these masterpieces of mineral painting when they reflect the sun- shine through a waving, rippling screen of crystal water is impossible of pictured reproduction.

And yet this phenomenon of terrace-building may be easily explained.   Nature has furnished here a series of object-lessons, which, viewed in the light of simple scientific facts, make all the mystery clear.   At our feet is a miniature formation where all the details of the grander terraces are minutely reproduced.   We see a tiny source of mineral water, a system of little bowls at various levels ; here already the construction of the terrace has begun.   The waters, as we know, contain calcareous matter ; as the water cools and evaporates, this substance is deposited ; cooling and evaporation naturally take place more rapidly at the outer rims of the bowls because by the time the water reaches them its temperature has decreased ; therefore the deposits at the edge are more quickly made, and thus the rims are gradually

THE BEGINNING OF A TERRACE

built up until the waters are forced to seek another place of
overflow, and recommence their work elsewhere. It has
been estimated that to increase the rim an inch in height
the water labors for a space of sixty days. The tinting is
caused by mineral substances brought with the waters from
the inner earth. But why seek to explain this seeming
miracle? It is enough that after years of toil the silent
forces will produce a thing of such enchanting beauty that
man's desire to investigate is lost in ecstasy of admiration.
It is enough for us that these yellows, browns, and purples
are harmoniously blended; that the still warm pools are
bluer than the fairest sky or deepest sea; that every line and
curve is to the eye as soft as a caress — it is enough that we
have felt the thrill born of the contemplation of the beautiful. What care we for calcareous deposits, evaporations,
sulphur stains, and iron oxides? Away with them.

Even Minerva, Goddess of Wisdom, whose name one terrace bears, here bids us admire rather than seek to understand. Nor is Minerva the only mythical deity honored here;
the name of Jupiter, the Father of the Gods, now dignifies

Photograph by F. Jay Haynes, St. Paul
MINERVA TERRACE

the grandest of the higher terraces. Born in
a pool which measures a full hundred feet
across, the waters of Jove's spring have
formed a terrace five acres in extent.
Surely the Greeks, had they possessed so
wonderful a piece of earth, would not
have exiled all their deities to
the peaks of barren moun-
tains. This region would
have been the Thunderer's
abode and that of his in-
numerable kindred. Now
I could lead you on for
hours from pool to spring,
from terrace to terrace.
I could compare the ter-
races with their broken
rainbows, to shattered spec-
tra, but all my words would
not suggest the half of what one

Photograph by F. Jay Haynes, St. Paul
LIBERTY CAP

glance reveals. I cannot but say, "Go thou and see."
But do not look for beauty in the full glare of noon. The
visitor who trudges over the terraces blinded by the crude
light of midday sees noth-   ing but dazzling
whites and dingy yel-   lows. The
softer light of even-
ing, or the glow
of sunrise best re-
veals the beauties
of the terraces.
We pause to
look at a huge cone,
which is called "Lib-
erty Cap"; it is the

ANGEL TERRACE

creation of an ancient spring,—a spring that may be said to have committed suicide by building up its crater to such a height that the waters, unable at last to reach the top and overflow, forsook this stately pile and went to labor at an architectural structure less ambitious.

Next morning, and, in fact, every morning during the season, an animated scene is witnessed at the landing-stage of the hotel. Five or six coaches dash up from the huge stables, and eager passengers take their places for the long drive of over one hundred and sixty miles around the park.

We cannot but admire the many excellences of the trans-portation outfit ; splendid Concord coaches, well-cared-for, solid and comfortable ; horses, well-groomed and strong ; drivers, as skilful as the western driver needs must be. Only one thing is there to criticize,—the utter absence of "local

THE START FROM MAMMOTH

color " in the rai-
ment of those
drivers. Why
has not the com-
pany seized this
splendid oppor-
tunity to preserve
a costume that
once was typical
of western life?
A corps of driv-
ers, not exactly
uniformed, but

A CONCORD COACH

dressed to fit their parts, in buckskins, broad-brimmed hats,
red shirts, and pistol-belts would be an innovation welcomed
by every traveler, for travelers demand the picturesque.

But as our skilful whip remarked, "Clothes don't make
the driver." Of this we are convinced long before the coach
enters the picturesque defile that forms the inner doorway to
the National Park. It is the famous portal known as "Golden
Gate," and the title Golden Gate is fitting in a double sense ;
the rocks are golden, while upon this last mile of road

OUR DRIVER

traversed much gold has been
expended — its construction
having cost the government
no less than $14,000. But
the road, alas, is badly engi-
neered, its grades are steep
enough to test the endurance
of the strongest horses, its
surface is buried in a small
Sahara of shifting sand and
dust impalpable as air. Fortunately a series of showers

preceded us and laid the dust along our way.   As our coach
toils slowly upward, as the murmur of the river grows fainter,
as the cliff-like cañon-walls draw nearer and nearer to one
another, we forget the steep grades of the heavy road in
admiration of scenes through which it leads us.   We are
but four miles from the springs, and yet we are a thousand
feet nearer the skies, two thousand feet above the railway
terminus, and seven thousand feet above the sea.

And presently the golden portals slowly open, revealing
to us a broad valley circled by mountains and dominated by
a cloudland, all of silver.   Far off we see the Gallatins, a
range whose average altitude above the sea is over 10,000
feet, but the great height of the park plateau reduces mountains to mere hills,
disappointing the
traveler who looks
for towering peaks
or Alpine scenery.
The great affinity
of the lightning for
one of the numer-
ous mountains that

GOLDEN GATE ROAD

surround this plateau led the discoverers to entitle it Electric
Peak. It is a sort of giant storage-battery ; explorers attempting to attain the summit have been baffled by electric forces,
which caused their fingers to prick and tingle and their hair
to stand on end.   They had, indeed, a shocking experience.

But leaving behind this huge Leyden jar, we approach, an
hour later, a unique feature, a mountain made of glass.
That black glistening mass is vitreous matter, obsidian or
volcanic glass, formed by the rapid cooling of a great wave
of lava.   Harder than stone, obsidian has long been a favorite material for the weapons of
primitive races, and yonder cliff
has furnished the aborigines with
countless arrowheads.

It has also furnished oppor-
tunities for some of the most
magnificent lies ever invented by
a prevaricating pioneer.   One of

GOLDEN GATE

Photograph by F. Jay Haynes, St. Paul

ELECTRIC PEAK

the early explorers became so ex-
asperated by the ridicule with
which his stories were received that he decided
to give his hearers
good and sufficient
cause for incredu-
lity. While hunt-
ing in this valley, so
runs his yarn, he
came upon a splen-
did elk, and being a

JWSTONE
JE

Photograph by F. Jay Haynes, St. Paul

OBSIDIAN CLIFF

3

Photograph by F. Jay Haynes, St. Paul
THE NEW ROAD

good shot he fired at long range. The elk did not even start; a second shot at closer range met with the same result. Therefore he ran toward the animal at full speed, until his career was suddenly arrested by crashing into a vertical wall of glass, so perfectly transparent that he had not noticed it. The elk was grazing peacefully upon the farther side. But not discouraged, our hunter made his way around the mountain only to find that the huge mass of glass had acted like a telescope, and had made him think that he was within a few rods of the game that in reality was twenty miles away.

As we drive on, we skirt a number of pretty lakes and finally, at noon, just as the thought of luncheon obtrudes itself, there flash into view the snow-white tents of "Larry's" famous lunch establishment. What traveler does not remember Larry Matthews and his canvas palace? Who can forget his cheery welcome when, lifting the ladies from the coach, he cries: "Glad to see you! Walk right up-stairs,— or would ye rather take the elevator?" And who

LARRY'S RESTAURANT

can forget the honest Irish face of landlord Larry Matthews?
His ready wit is remarkable.   Every day he is expected

A LEAP FOR LUNCHEON

to be funny from 11 to 2 o'clock, during which hours he must not only delight the inbound tourists, but carefully avoid repeating himself

in the presence of those outward bound who lunch here for the second time. He 's hard to catch, however, for his bright sallies come just as freely as do his smiles. As an example of Larry's quickness, there was in our party an Italian gentleman we laughingly called the Count. "Ah, Count," uttered Larry, "glad to meet you; but

LARRY MATTHEWS

you know a dollar 's all that 's
a count in this café.''

We never know what
we are eating at Larry's
busy table d'hôte.
He never gives us
time to think about
the food.   He is
able to make the
people laugh so
much and eat so
little that the com-
pany should meet all
his demands for an in-
crease of salary.   A lady
asks for a glass of milk.
''Drive in the cow!'' shouts

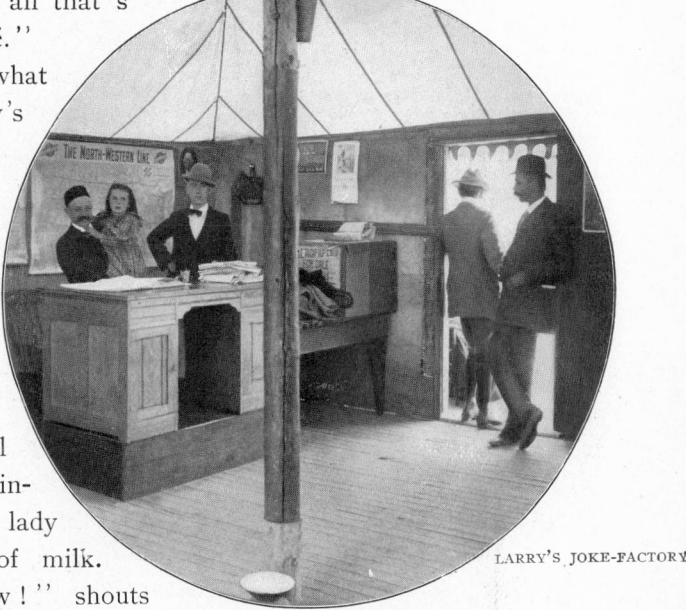

LARRY'S JOKE-FACTORY

Larry.   ''A drink of water, if you please,'' murmurs a pretty

IN LARRY'S ''CAFAY''

"CALAMITY" IN SCOUTING COSTUME

miss; and Larry with deep solicitude inquires, "Wad ye like it hot or cold?" And then if one looks wistfully upon the butter or the sauce, he quickly reassures you with the declaration that "there's no extra charge for flies and dust, —always on the bill-of-fare,— a standing order." This joke, like the dish referred to, is "a standing order"; but although we lunched four times at Larry's, we seldom caught him putting old cylinders in his

"CALAMITY-JANE"

phonograph of fun. The eruptions of laughter that occur every day with greatest regularity at Larry's, certainly cause as much genuine amusement as any of the spoutings of the neighboring geysers. It was at Larry's that we met the original, Simon-pure "Calamity-Jane," who twenty years ago was famous as a woman-scout, and served our generals faithfully in many of the Indian wars. As we ride away from Larry's and the laughter dies away, we begin to hear a

Photograph by F. Jay Haynes, St. Paul

THE BLACK GROWLER

roaring as of rushing steam, and presently we are halted
by the sentinel of the geyser regions, who holds aloft a pillar
of hissing vapor to warn us that we are approaching danger-

Photograph by F. Jay Haynes, St. Paul
GIBBON CAÑON

ous ground.   We could not, if we would, ignore the Black
Growler, whose gruff songs of greeting and farewell will
haunt the tourist's memory for years.   Day and night,
unceasingly, the growler utters his deep, sullen roar.   But
why called *Black* Growler no one seems to know.   Perhaps
some blind man may have named it ; for just as to the blind a
blare of trumpets suggests a brilliant red, so to us, if we shut
our eyes, the roar of this great safety-valve sounds *black*.

As the other features of the Norris Basin are reproduced on a much grander scale elsewhere, we do not linger, but drive on amid the beauties of the Gibbon Cañon, where forest and stream combine to charm the eye. And do you realize the importance of the trees and waters of the Yellowstone? The park is a forest-covered region, completely isolated in the midst of a vast tract of treeless deserts. In it there are no fewer than thirty-six lakes, and twenty-five waterfalls, while its streams and brooks are numberless. It is a well known fact that even at the season of low water this generous region sends forth a refreshing flood into the surrounding parched states. No one can estimate the loss that would ensue should this supply be cut off or diminished. Yet the possibility exists. Destroy, or permit the destruction of, these glorious forests that cover almost nine tenths of the park, and the land will become a barren waste. These miles and miles and miles of piny growth insure the life of all the lakes and streams by preventing a too rapid melting of the snow and by luring the rain from the vapory clouds. The government has most wisely adopted sufficient measures for the preservation of the park's green mantle,

CYCLISTS

but eternal vigilance is the price of the security ; our Federal troops who play the part of fireman within the National Park are often called upon to fight fierce battles with the forest flames.

En route once more, a cloud of happy cyclists flits by our coach. Here my cycling friends will ask, "Would you advise a wheel-tour through the park?" Yes, and no. No,

IN DIVIDED SKIRTS   for the rider who expects to roll through the Rockies as easily as over city boulevards and parkways. Yes, for the man who thinks fatigue essential to enjoyment, who does not object to roads four inches deep in sand, who can ride up heavy grades, and whose temper is as well trained as his legs. To those who would ride around the park astride a saddle, I commend the plan adopted by these two young ladies, for

if the girl in bloomers is not seen scorching through the wilderness a-wheel, she is not absent altogether — she has merely a change of mount. These sensible eques-

A HUMBLE FOUR-IN-HAND

triennes are but types of scores who, like them, tour the park in divided skirts. They are, as a rule, members of some itinerant camping-party, their mothers, fathers, aunts and uncles, brothers and sisters, preceding or following them in great white prairie-schooners, of which

IN CAMP

large fleets are tacking to and fro across the park in all directions. These people do not patronize the great hotels. They carry tents, supplies, cooking-stoves, and cameras. They come from every state. We talked with people from California, Texas, Michigan, and Maine. In one week during our visit two hundred and seventy-five campers registered at the military post at the entrance of the park ; every person entering the park must register and leave his firearms in charge of the guards, unless he prefers to have the lock of every weapon sealed, the seal not to be broken until he passes out again. If the soldiers who here

CAMPERS

serve as park po-
licemen find a
camper with an
unsealed gun,
they are at liberty
to suppose that
the sight of some
huge elk or grace-
ful deer has been
too much for him.
The broken seal
may cost him a
fine of one thou-
sand dollars, or a
long sojourn in
the stone house
at Fort Yellow-
stone. The following queries recently appeared in a daily
paper : "How large is the park?" "Is it surrounded by a
fence?" "What is the fence made of?" My answers are :
"The park is sixty-five miles long
by fifty-five miles wide." "It
is surrounded by a fence."
"The fence is made of
flesh and blood, endur-
ance and courage, and
covered with the uni-
form of the United
States cavalry."

As we ride on,
we meet other trav-
elers more economical,
who, dispensing with
tents, wagons, and stoves,

"DON'T TAKE MY PICTURE!"

reduce their baggage to such a point that one or two pack horses suffice for transport.   We saw one lonely camper with his "baggage cars" coupled by neck and tail in a simple but ingenious way. The complete outfit of another enthusiastic traveler reveals no suggestion of luxury.   It consists of a canvas sleeping-bag, and a few boxes of supplies. He tells us that it has long been his ambition to see the great west, and that the hard times of 1896 convinced him that it would be cheaper to travel and enjoy himself than to remain in business; accordingly, with two horses and this slender outfit, he set out from Cheyenne with the intention of visiting every point of interest between the Missouri and the Pacific Coast.   He travels leisurely, and although he confesses to

AMP FOLLOWER

A TRAIN OF "BAGGAGE-CARS"

occasional spells of loneli-
ness, he says that he thor-
oughly enjoys his absolute
freedom and would change
places with no man.   His
journey costs him on an average just fifty cents a day.

But while we have been
discussing passing travelers,
our coach has brought us
to the Upper Geyser Basin,
where the geysers like gigantic censers are wafting

ON THE MARCH

their vapory incense skyward.   A geyser basin is an area
where the crust of this great volcanic region is thinnest.   In
venturing out upon its surface, which in places gives back
hollow echoes to our tread, we feel
that we are very near indeed to
the infernal fires.   Everything
about us tends to excite
both timidity and awe.
"Unearthly" is the best
word to describe the
scene, and as we pick
our way amid steam-
ing pools, as columns
of steam and boiling
water suddenly rear
themselves beside, in
front of, or behind us,
as gusts of heated air
fan our faces and the
sound of hissing vapors
fills the ear, we may be

AN ECONOMICAL OUTFIT

THE CASTLE AND THE BEEHIVE GEYSERS

Photograph by F. Jay Haynes, St. Paul

Photograph by F. Jay Haynes, St. Paul

THE FOUNTAIN HOTEL

pardoned if a sense of the supernatural overpowers us,
if we falter for a moment until familiarity with these

Photograph by F. Jay Haynes, St. Paul

THE FOUNTAIN GEYSER

4

phenomena shall give us confidence. The theory of geyser
action advanced by Bunsen and accepted by the scientific
world is not difficult to comprehend. A geyser crater is
usually a deep, well-like fissure filled with water; it is of
unknown depth; near the bottom there are volcanic fires or
heated rocks that act upon the lower sections of the watery

Photograph by F. Jay Haynes, St. Paul
CRATER OF OLD FAITHFUL

column enclosed in this deep narrow well. We know that
water under heavy pressure must be raised to a higher temperature before it will boil than water that is merely being
heated in an open caldron. Therefore the lower sections
of the water column, before reaching their boiling-point, are
heated to such a degree that were the pressure not so great,
ebullition would certainly result. Imagine, then, this state

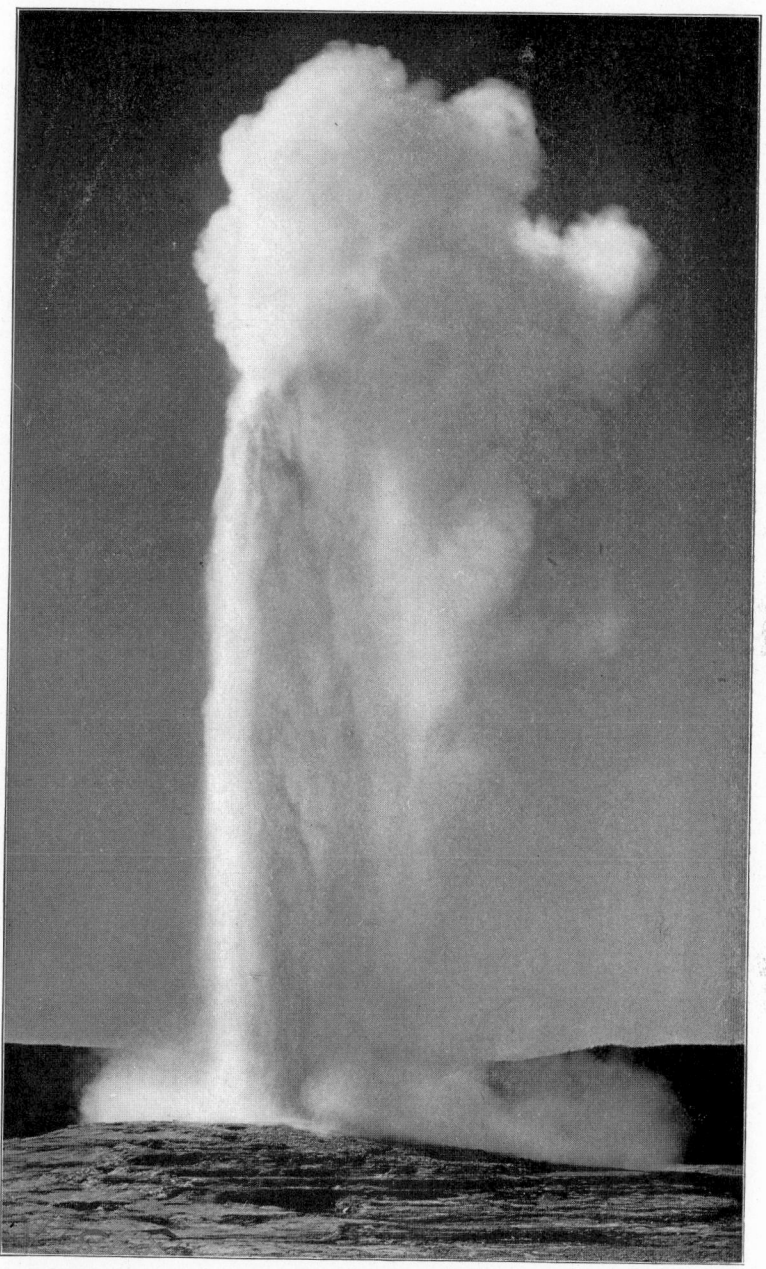

Photograph by F. Jay Haynes, St. Paul

AN HOURLY SPECTACLE

of things : water which is hot enough to boil under normal
conditions, but prevented from boiling and from producing
steam by the immense pressure to which it is subjected.
Then imagine that a little of the water nearest to the subter-

Photograph by F. Jay Haynes, St. Paul
WATER AND STEAM

ranean fires becomes hot enough to boil in spite of the pressure. A little steam is thus produced. This rises, disturbs,
and slightly lifts the superincumbent column of cooler water.
The pressure, which alone prevents ebullition, is thus relieved.

What then occurs? The vast mass of superheated water deep in the well suddenly finds itself not, as before, below its boiling-point, but far above it, and without waiting to boil it instantaneously flashes into steam, and the cooler water resting above it is shot forth as from a cannon's mouth to awe mankind, to tell him of the terrible unalterability of Nature's laws.

Thus we may understand the great irregularity of the eruptions. So many factors are to be considered — the depth, diameter, and direction of the geyser tube, the proximity of the heated rocks, and the workings of the water system which refills the tube, whether by infiltration of rain or river water, or by the flow of subterranean springs. The marvel is, not that the moment of these glorious displays cannot be accurately named, but that it can be even approximately surmised. One geyser, only, makes any pretense to punctuality. It has been named on this account "Old Faithful." Regularly every hour it performs its task of entertaining tourists. It merits the gratitude of those who have not time to wait upon the whims of its eccentric neighbors.

While waiting with an expectant group of visitors, one overhears many amusing remarks. Some tourists, led astray by one of Larry's jokes, ask at what time they are going to "grease the geyser." And this expression, "greasing the geyser," refers to a former custom of putting soap into the crater to make the geyser spout before its time. This practice of soaping is now prohibited, for it eventually destroys the action of the geyser. The fact

WAITING FOR AN ERUPTION

Photograph by F. Jay Haynes, St. 'Paul

OLD FAITHFUL

that soaping would advance the hour of eruption was discovered quite by accident.   A Chinese laundryman who had
found the hot pools a great convenience in his business, one
day mixed his suds in the wrong hole.   His pigtailed head
escaped by miracle as a charge of shirts, collars, and cuffs
was fired skyward with tremendous force.

As the moment of the eruption approaches, an impatient
visitor, who has been watching the steam ascending from the
crater, demands, "Well, when does she bust?" but on ob-
serving the tightness of the clothes of the corpulent ques-
tioner, it seems to be a close question as to which will
"bust" the sooner—the geyser or the gentleman.   At last,
however, some one cries, "Look out!—there she goes!"
There is a backward rush of dazed spectators, and upward in
a mass of glittering glory the contents of the tube is lifted,

forming a dazzling pillar of rising
and falling water, surrounded
by its flowing draperies of
steam.   This is repeated
every hour with but the
slightest variations.
Here is a water-clock
older than that of the
Greeks, and it marks
time as perfectly to-
day as when the divine
clockmaker first put to-
gether its more than mys-
terious mechanism.   That
monument of water is one
hundred and fifty feet in
height.   It stands there
apparently undiminished
for seven minutes, and

"WELL, WHEN DOES SHE BUST?"

Photograph by F. Jay Haynes, St. Paul
THE GIANT

in these seven minutes no less than one and a half million gallons of boiling water are shot forth. In one day Old Faithful furnishes more water than would be used for the needs of a city of three hundred thousand people. Nor is this all, for this is but one of the hundred geysers which, day and night, summer and winter, are rising thus like ghostly sentinels to see that all is well in Nature's Wonderland, and then returning again to oft-broken slumbers.

It seems as if the other geysers, conscience stricken by the punctuality and frequency of Old Faithful's exhibitions, individually were

to make up for their long periods of laziness by giving
superior displays when their turns arrive.

Excelsior, the grandest of them all, spends seven or more
years in preparation, and then begins a series of imposing
outbursts.   A mighty cliff of living water rises from a boiling
lake, and as often as the waters fall, they are hurled again
into the air.   Though its form is ever changing, the cliff of
water stands there in seeming permanency, until at last the
unseen forces weaken and the glorious vision vanishes.   The
level of the river that flows near the crater of Excelsior is
raised several inches after every outburst of this great geyser,
which in one eruption ejects more water than could be
thrown up by the combined forces of all the other geysers in
the basin.   Unfortunately all is quiet here on the day of our
visit.   The last preceding display occurred in 1892.   Beautiful as are the manifestations of the forces of nature when

Photograph by F. Jay Haynes, St. Paul

CRATER OF EXCELSIOR

acting upon the clear, deep pools, they become ridiculous or
fantastic when mud is substituted in the craters for the
crystal waters.   Here in the mammoth "Paint Pots" nature
plays a joke upon us.   In one caldron is a mass of mortar-

Photograph by F. Jay Haynes, St. Paul
EXCELSIOR IN ERUPTION

like mud, which during unknown ages has been in a state of
ebullition.   Up through the slimy matter rise tiny puffs of
steam, each one ejecting, with a nauseating flop, a tiny spout
of what looks like vanilla or strawberry ice-cream, half
melted.   The shapes which are momentarily assumed by
these expectorations of the clayey slush are grotesque to
such a point that lookers-on are frequently convulsed with
laughter.   The word "grotesque" describes the Paint Pots;

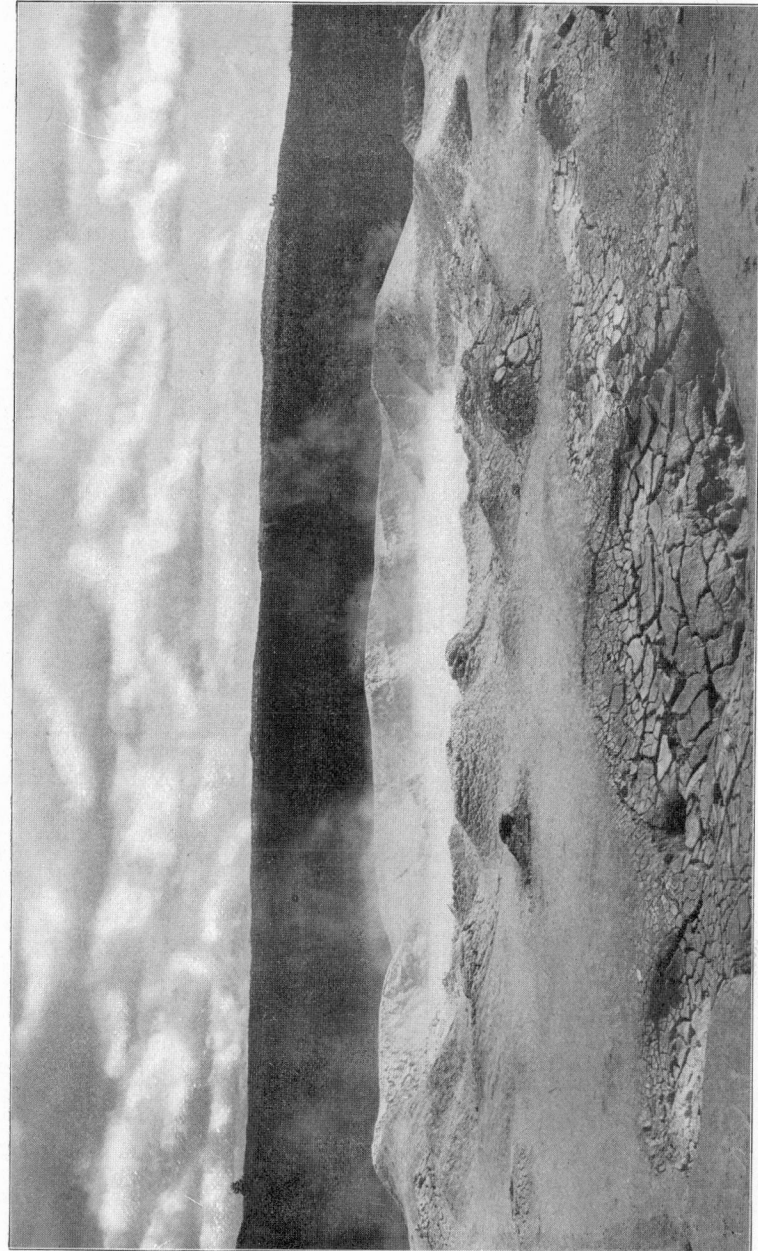

THE MAMMOTH " PAINT POTS "

Photograph by F. Jay Haynes, St. Paul

THE UPPER GEYSER BASIN

wonderful, marvelous, and grand are the adjectives we use
in speaking of the geysers; but when we would tell of the
Morning Glory Spring, a still, warm pool of deepest blue, the
word "beautiful" is the only one that rises to our lips. Those
who have never looked into its depths will smile incredulously, and being shown a colored photograph of the spring,

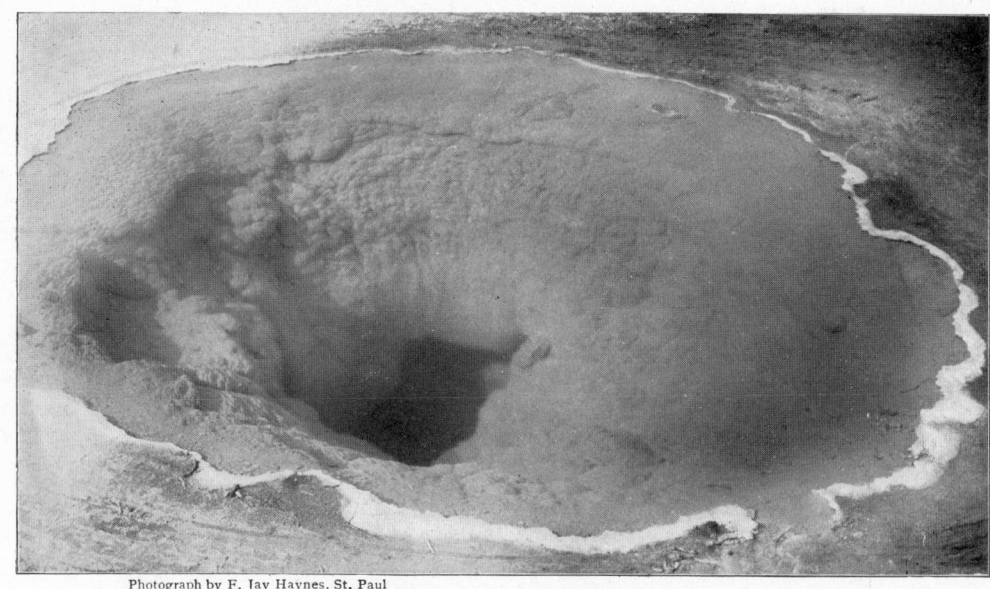

Photograph by F. Jay Haynes, St. Paul

MORNING GLORY SPRING

say that photographer and artist have told a most transparent
lie. But eyes that have been treated to this bath of beauty

THE GROTTO GEYSER

will tell you that no photographic lens can there be substituted for the human eye, that not by any painter's pigment may the exquisite tones of blue be reproduced. The lining of the crater is of snow-white deposit, the water itself is colorless, and yet the illusion of blueness is intense and persists even on gray cloudy days. It seems as if it had been vouchsafed to us to peer into the deep, placid soul of nature. Reluctantly turning from the contemplation of these cerulean depths, we find ourselves again

LOOKING INTO
THE MUD VOLCANO

upon the inter·minable sandy road cut through the piny forest. No correct impression of the Yellowstone and its wonders can be imparted unless scenes are linked together by sections of that long, long road on which the traveler must spend seven hours every day.

THE BUTTERFLY

I mean the traveler who insists on rushing through the park on schedule time, in five and a half days, not because he is compelled to, but because he has been told that it is possible.

We cannot praise the undue expedition with which the average traveler rushes through our Wonderland. Few, if any, take time for more than a mere glance at the lakelet that lies in a little hollow on the crest of the continental divide. And yet that lily-dotted pond merits our thoughtful consideration and will richly repay the visitor.

We are in the Rocky Mountains near the apex of our continent. That placid sheet of water is therefore wooed by two mighty suitors,—the Atlantic and the Pacific,—and, undecided but impartial, she bestows her favors on them both

A LAKELET THAT FEEDS TWO OCEANS

Photograph by F. Jay Haynes, St. Paul

SHOSHONE LAKE AND THE TETONS

alike; and when she weeps for love of both, one tear may trickle down the cheek kissed by her western lover, the Pacific, while another salutes the outstretched arms of the Atlantic, in the Gulf of Mexico. From this point onward, the dash down-grade is thrillingly exciting; our four horses swing us at a spanking pace around curves and past a score of splendid points of view. Far away to the south, outside the limits of the park, we see the three great Teton Peaks rising as if in protest at their exclusion from our Wonderland—as if by an unwearying appeal they would compel the government to reconsider that unsatisfactory southern boundary line, to move it a few miles farther south, and thus add to the park a feature that it lacks, a range of alpine grandeur. Nearer, and well within the limits of the park, we see the beautiful Shoshone Lake, while all around us rise the wooded slopes of the apparently insignificant range that forms the backbone of our land — the Continental Divide.

Photograph by F. Jay Haynes, St. Paul
LAKE YELLOWSTONE AND MOUNT SHERIDAN

Still following the down-trending road, we reach some hours later the shores of that great silent reservoir of icy waters, Lake Yellowstone. With a shore-line more than one hundred miles in length, with an altitude of almost a mile and a half above the sea, there are but few lakes in the world that surpass Lake Yellowstone in area and elevation. One or two lakes in the Andes of Peru, one or two in the scarce explored regions of Tibet are its only rivals.

Around Lake Yellowstone rise mountains from ten to fifteen thousand feet in height, and yet these mountains, because we are already almost eight thousand feet above sea-level, do not seem to us more lofty than a range of hills. The mere knowledge that a mountain is of immense altitude does not impress one half so much as the apparent height

LAKE YELLOWSTONE

of lesser peaks. Thus Mount Washington, in New Hampshire, with its mere six thousand feet of visible elevation, seems grander to us than these giants which have almost thrice its height. Yet bring hither our favorite New England peak, bury it beneath the lake, its base at the sea-level, and then where would the dizzily perched Summit House find itself? It would be occupied by trout and other finny guests, while the instruments of the Mount Washington observatory would be rusting more than a thousand feet below these waters. Nay, the summit would not rise high enough even to pierce the muddy bottom of Lake Yellowstone.

THE HOTEL AT THE LAKE

Were this courageous little steamer on which we cross the lake to prolong its excursion on this same plane of altitude eastward from the Rockies, it would sail across our continent almost eight thousand feet above our cities, accompanied

THE ONLY STEAMER

by fleets of clouds; it would cross the broad Atlantic, meeting no obstacle until its prow grated upon the icy slopes of the Alps or Pyrenees. We may not take this flying trip, however, but shall steam on toward a little island where there are confined a few tame buffalo; the only buffalo we may hope to see, for in the summer the wild herd inhabiting the

CAPTIVE BUFFALO

park seldom presents itself to tourists' eyes.   But the days
of the wild bison are numbered, although it is protected
by the strong arm of the law; there remains to-day only a
meager band, yearly decimated, and doomed to ultimate ex-
tinction.   The traveler who will brave the rude winter of
these altitudes may be rewarded by a sight of four or five

Photograph by F. Jay Haynes, St. Paul

ELK

wild buffalo in full retreat across the snow-covered open
stretches.   But a visit to the park in winter is no simple
matter; snow then lies from ten to twenty feet upon the
level and is piled mountain-high in the ravines.   Yet a
winter tour is possible, though at the cost of sufferings and
perils which few men will care to pay.   The cold at that
period is frightful.   In the words of an intrepid photographer

who has made several midwinter tours in the Yellowstone,
"When it was only ten degrees below, we called it a warm
day.   We had been accustomed, during our two-hundred-
mile snow-shoe journey, to a temperature of fifty-two degrees
below zero."   And there are men who every winter hiber-
nate in the big empty hotels of the park, for reasons
that insurance companies best understand.   The manager

Photograph by F. Jay Haynes, St. Paul
FIREHOLE CASCADES

of the hotel at the Grand Cañon, with his wife, spends
nine long, lonely months in the snow-bound caravansary,
there being miles of snowy nothingness between him and the
world.   But he is not a prisoner; he often glides out of a
third-story window on his Norwegian skees, and then as lightly
as a sea-gull he skims down and away across white snow-
fields, which sustain him some twenty feet above the level of
old earth.   He has looked upon scenes whose fascinations he
avers are ample recompense for what to us would seem

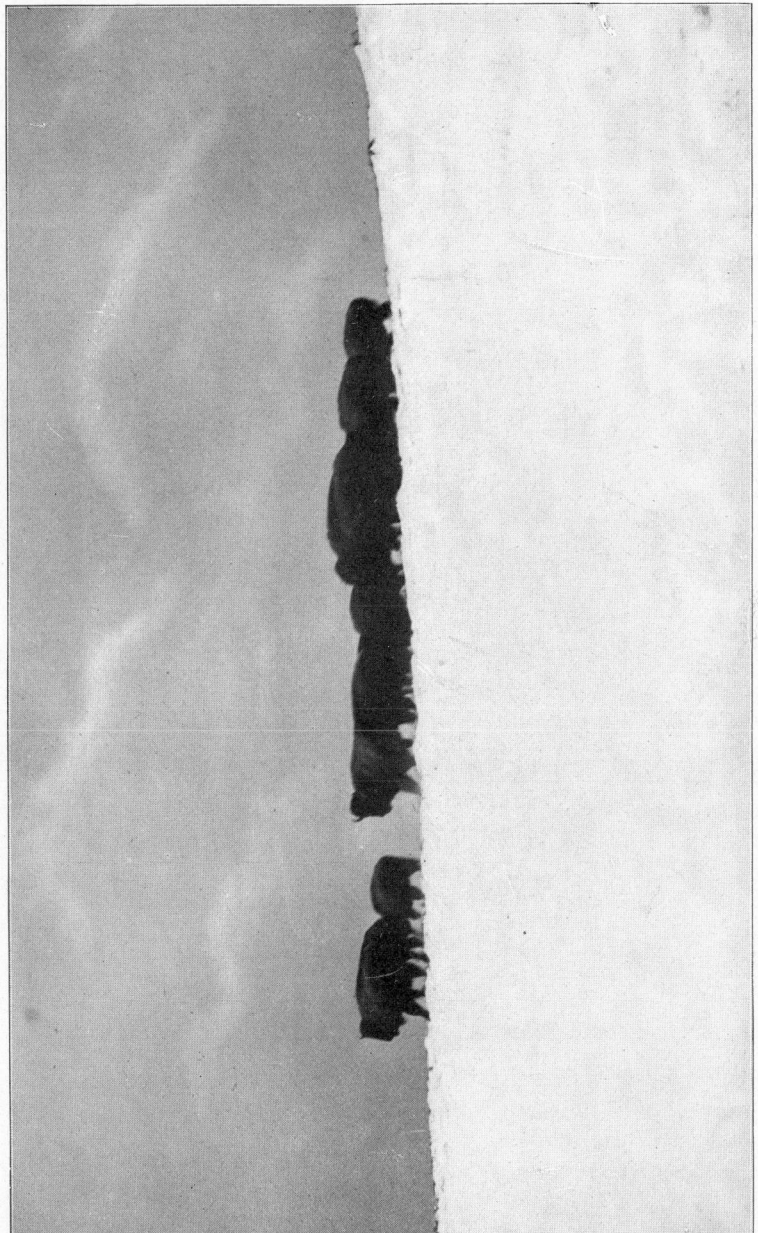

WINTER VISITORS

Photograph by F. Jay Haynes, St. Paul

almost a living death.   Think of it : two people spending
here a winter of two hundred and fifty days, each day so
like another that the march of time is imperceptible.

But ere these thoughts shall chill us to the bone, let us
return to summer sunshine by the lake.   The view of the lake
reminds us that I have not mentioned what is to some the
chief charm of these waters,—the fact that they are literally
swarming with fish, so eager to be caught that skill is not
required.   Naturally, Yellowstone fish-stories are like other
things in this region,—the most remarkable of their kind, for
the reason that unlike other fish-stories, they are absolutely
true.   No exaggeration is needed to add color to them.   Let
me prove it to you.   In the picture you may see my friend,
after casting his line into the icy waters of the lake, dipping
the finny prey into the depths of a spring of boiling water.
What a convenience for the hungry traveler !—his Friday
breakfast kept cool and fresh in a vast natural refrigerator
until it pleases him to fish it out, flop it into a natural kettle

COOKING A CATCH

and, without budging, cook it on the spot.   You are incredu-
lous, because, alas ! truth and the finny tribe have no affinity.
And I will confess that, although containing many ingredi-
ents of truth, my tale is not a wholly honest one, for

MOUNT WASHBURNE

although this culinary feat is performed by tourists every day,
in our case the fish could not be made to bite, the steamer
was whistling her last warning, and — dare I confess it ? —
impelled by photographic necessities, I hastened to the

kitchen in the luncheon-tent
near by, purchased a miserable trout, and hung its stiff,
cold corpse upon our dan-
gling, disappointed hook.

After this confession, as a
proof of my regard for truth,
can you refuse to believe my
other stories ?   Here is one to
test your confidence : There
is in the park a river in which
geyser waters overflow.   As

ON MOUNT WASHBURNE

the hot water rests upon the surface, the cold, trout-swarm-
ing river is, as it were, covered with a stratum of boiling water,
and fish caught in its depths may be cooked on the way out!

Leaving the lake, let us follow the swift-flowing but placid
river to the culmination of our journey, the Grand Cañon of
the Yellowstone. Strange,—is it not?—that the approach
should promise so little: a level valley, a ribbon of green
water, and in the distance the shadowy forms of Mounts
Washburne and Dunraven.

But before we turn to the consideration of the cañon, let
me recall briefly an excursion over Mount Washburne to
Yancey's ranch—a horseback trip that may be made as an
alternative to the return to Mammoth Hot Springs by the
coach-road. The ascent of Mount
Washburne is not difficult, and it
calls for neither great endurance nor
daring horsemanship. The trail, although in places indistinct, is easy
and secure as mountain-trails go.

AT THE SUMMIT

The view from the summit is not especially striking to one accustomed to mountain scenery of regions more broken and picturesque, but the exhilaration of the ride and the resulting appetites are ample compensations for the effort. A visit to "Uncle John Yancey's" ranch is an experience that will be remembered but which will not be repeated.

YANCEY HIMSELF

A comic writer might find food for profitable study in the peculiarities of Uncle John, but the ordinary traveler will find neither palatable food nor decent accommodations while at the old man's "Hotel." The tenderfoot should not remark the unwashed condition of the two historic glasses into which the proprietor pours the welcoming libation of "Kentucky tea," for it is Yancey's boast that his whisky glasses have never been polluted by the contact of

YANCEY'S

so alien a liquid as water. That water is not held in good repute at Yancey's is evidenced by the location and condition of the "bathing establishment" maintained for the inconvenience of guests who are so perverted as to require more than the pail that serves the needs of the habitués of the primitive caravansary. On the whole it is wiser to leave the park with the impressions of its glories undimmed by memories of Yancey's Ranch.

GRUB

The approach to the cañon from the lake is commonplace indeed, yet between us and those unimpressive mountains toward which we drive, lies one of the grandest sights on which man has ever looked — one of the great things of the world. The mountains are largely forest-clad ; for miles on both sides of the cañon there stretch away great areas of timber that soften every outline of the landscape, give it a regularity, a velvety smoothness, that ill prepare the traveler

ONE OF YANCEY'S
BOARDERS

for the chaotic awfulness of that on which he is about to look. It is as if nature had striven by every means to enhance the sublime surprise that she reserves behind this curtain of deep green. Yet, lest we should be stricken blind and dumb by the full, instantaneous revelation of the glory of the lower cañon, let us look first upon the milder beauty of the upper gorge. Into it leaps the river, in a plunge of a hundred feet or more, then on it rushes between gray-wooded walls, its waters greener than the pines, or, being churned to foam, whiter than snow. Follow me down to the river-bank; no danger need be

THE BATHING ESTABLISHMENT

THE UPPER YELLOWSTONE

feared; beauty, not danger, lurks below. Here for a moment the waters seem to curb their eagerness, as if the drops which have journeyed long in company would bid farewell to

Photograph by F. Jay Haynes, St. Paul
THE GRAND CAÑON HOTEL

one another, before, in the confusion of their final leap, they are forever separated or dispersed in spray.   Dare we now in imagination follow them? Nay, we are almost tempted to follow bodily, so great is the fascination of the flood, as with

6

A PATH TO THE BRINK

IN THE UPPER GORGE

THE UPPER CAÑON OF THE YELLOWSTONE

a calm deliberate swiftness, like that of a mighty eagle
swooping upon its prey, it glides as lightly as the wind over
the brink, and plunges toward the center of the world.   Instantly, as if by powerful enchantment, it is transformed
from a greenish serpent into a bridal veil of purest white.
We are assisting at the nuptials of awfulness and beauty.
But to appreciate the full solemnity of it all, one must hear
the ceaseless roar, like the anthem of the eternal choir, and
feel the cool spray-like aspersions, as of the holy water.

But having seen beauty fall into the arms of awfulness,
we will look upon the land in which they are to dwell together while the brief honeymoon endures.   Then close your
eyes, turn them toward the east, open them, and suppress a

BRINK OF THE LOWER FALLS

gasp of admiration if you can! Our first impression is one
of overwhelming surprise. The cañon is so much vaster
than we thought. Its coloring is more vivid than we ever
dreamed it could be. It seems like a mine of precious
stones, uncovered to amaze and dazzle the sun itself. The
river has already cut down through this mine of color more
than a thousand feet, yet the vein seems to be inexhaustible.
The rocky mass of the plateau is decomposed to unknown
depths ; the chemic products resulting from that decomposi-
tion produce the color ; the rains, the flow of water from
subterranean springs, and the winds that sweep through the
cañon have helped to blend the tints, until the walls appear
as if draped with the tatters of some gorgeous rainbow.

THE CAÑON OF THE YELLOWSTONE FROM THE FALLS

MAJESTY!

AMID THE PINES

But there are other points of vantage from which even more stupendous vistas are revealed. To reach them we must turn back and climb up in and through the woods that clothe the slope of the upper cañon. The quick transitions from light to shade, from free space to the seclusion of the forest, are delightful. In the soft gloom of the wood we may repose our eyes wearied with too much glory. Overcome by the unseizable vastness of the cañon, we turn with pleasure to the contemplation of little things which elsewhere would have no interest for us. For hours in these woods I have watched the chipmunks, busy, saucy little animals, which being unmolested here are so tame that when I sat quite motionless they would approach, sit on the other end of the same log, and try to enter into conversation.

One day, however, I encountered upon this steep, narrow path a number of strange beings, so wholly out of keeping with the scene that I could not believe my eyes. They were members of a military cycle expedition—eight soldiers from

the colored regiment of Fort Mis-
soula, in Montana, who under
the command of young Lieutenant Moss, successfully
accomplished a journey of
over one thousand miles
a-wheel. Each man
carried from sixty to
seventy pounds of bag-
gage ; a complete camp-
equipment, tents, poles,
and blankets, supplies,
dishes, cooking-uten-
sils, and provisions, in
addition to the heavy
arms and ammunition.
Thus handicapped, these men

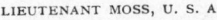

LIEUTENANT MOSS, U. S. A.   rode sometimes ninety miles a day

DIFFICULT BIKING

A COMPLETE CAMP ON WHEELS

over western roads that are a disgrace to our civilization. No wonder that to them the roads within the park seemed almost perfect by comparison.

But as we find ourselves upon the road that skirts the cañon brink, we must confess that the park roads, though not so very bad, are, when compared to European roads, disgracefully inferior. Nowhere is a system of splendid highways more needed, for railroads

THE ROAD TO THE RIM

have been permanently barred out. Let Congress indulge
in a wise expenditure some may call extravagance, and make
the Yellowstone a park in fact as well as in name.

Yes, as we peer into the piny labyrinths, which lie between us and the cañon precipice, we feel that here nature
has done so much that man should not refuse to do his
share. Nature provides a feast of beauty ; she asks only
that man shall make the banquet hall accessible. Let us
hope that it will be done ; that the future will see here in our
park hundreds of miles of splendid avenues, which with
graceful curves and gradual inclines will lead the people of
many lands into this wilderness. Beginning at the Springs,
the throngs of future visitors will view the marvels of the

A FOREST POOL

park with an increasing wonder and enthusiasm, and will be brought here to this forest, on the verge of the abyss, prepared by what they have already seen to draw aside these piny screens and look with reverence and wonder upon the grandest sight of all, this overwhelming acme to their journey, the Grand Cañon of the Yellowstone.

From Lookout Point the Great Fall looks almost insignificant ; yet its waters drop almost twice as far as those of huge Niagara. What seems from a distance a ribbon of white spray is in truth a stream seventy-four feet in width and three hundred and sixty feet in length.

Below us is a pure white mound of formation, not of snow as we at first imagine ; but snow is not a stranger

THE GRAND CAÑON OF THE YELLOWSTONE

here ; upon the contrary it is almost a regular inhabitant, for
in the Yellowstone they say there are only three seasons and
they are called "July, and August, and Winter." And
winter is the most impressive of them all.   Then no array of
startling color strikes the eye.   Then all is cold and still.
The cañon sleeps beneath a covering of dazzling whiteness,

IN THE YELLOWSTONE FOREST

and a great solitude is over all.   For nine long months the
cañon slumbers thus.   Then, waked by the first kiss of summer, she gently lays aside, one by one, the robes of white in
which she has been sleeping, dons the most gorgeous of her
thousand dresses, and welcomes the return of her long-absent
lover, the sunshine of the glorious summer days.

Photograph by F. Jay Haynes, St. Paul

POINT LOOKOUT

From the brink we cannot always see the depth of the
cañon. "Red Rock," and pinnacles of other hues obstruct
our view, while from the cañon walls great screens, like
wings on a theater-stage, have been pushed out to cut the
lines of sight and add confusion and disorder to the scene.
These delicately tinted screens are as beautiful in color as

Photograph by F. Jay Haynes, St. Paul
WINTER

they are strange in form. We find here reproduced the
Gothic forms of Occidental architecture, with an opulence of
color that is more than Oriental. Hundreds of Gothic spires,
—feudal castles, too, with fantastic crenelations, all these
are here. Nor is the masonry of cold, gray rock; instead,
the walls are all aflame with amber, amethyst, and jasper.
Nor are these castle-ruins few in number; they seem in truth

7

innumerable.   Let us look deeper ; there far, far down are other detached spires apparently floating in the dimness of a lower world.   And do you realize the magnitude of some of these great natural minarets?   Yonder tower, of a dull garnet color, would dwarf a modern office-building of twelve stories.   Do you realize the height of the great wall that

FROM THE BRINK

rises in the shadow far beyond?   To illustrate its height, take four great buildings, each like the Masonic Temple of Chicago, and pile them one upon another.   Then place in the cañon the towering structure thus created, the ground floor resting at the river's level.   Do you believe that the roof garden would surpass the summit of that wall?   If so,

PINNACLES AND TOWERS

you are mistaken ; the people gathered there would have to look upward to see us standing on the cañon's brink.

Let us now drive on until we reach the one point from which the playful traveler is permitted to send great rocks rolling and bounding down the steep sides of the mighty ditch. We drop a boulder over the precipice. At first the stone rolls down the smooth sandy slope, then, on reaching a narrow defile some hundreds of feet below, it begins to bound back and forth in zigzags between the bases of the jutting pinnacles. At every concussion the big rolling

TOSSING THE BOULDER

stone detaches huge masses of decomposed rock from the cliffs, and these
join in the mad downward rush
by hundreds.   Meantime we
follow with fascinated eyes
the boulder's wild career as
in leaps of several hundred
feet it nears its watery destination.   But it seems as if
it never would arrive, so great
is the distance it must travel.
Smaller and smaller it appears to
grow, until at last the boulder, looking

WATCHING IT ROLL

to us like a tiny
pebble, plunges
soundlessly into
the greenish flood
of the Yellow-
stone and disap-
pears.   So excit-
ing is this game
of tenpins that we
search for other
rocks ; but the
brink has been
well cleared by
former players.
We find just one
stone left, the
only one that has
not been rolled
down the slope by
tourists ; nor will

MYSTERIOUS DEPTHS

it be until our race becomes far sturdier than it is to-day,
for that one remaining boulder is more than fifteen feet in
diameter.   It is remarkable not only for its size, but also for
its complete isolation.   It is the only piece of granite in this
valley.   Its nearest neighbor lies more than twenty miles
away.   How came it here? we ask; and science answers
that it was stranded here by some prehistoric river of ice,
left to bear eternal witness to the existence of glaciers in this
region.   It is a mighty mile-stone on the highway of geology.
It marks the close of an epoch in the history of our terres-
trial sphere.   It records the abdication of a glacial king.

But the wondrous beauty of the forest cannot keep us
long away from the Grand Cañon.   We are involuntarily

A PERILOUS POSITION

THE GIFT OF A GLACIER

drawn to the very brink. Who is there that cannot understand the fascination of the cañon ? No one can look into its depths, as we do now from Inspiration Point, and not have an overwhelming desire to go down and solve the mystery of its great beauty and its grandeur. Who is there that does not envy the eagles that dwell upon the pinnacles, and are free to soar in slow, grand curves between these gorgeous walls, free to descend and drink of the rushing waters far below ; free to survey the scene from points of view which man will never reach. One mystery, however, never can be solved ; that of the perfect blending of these colors. All hues are there, spread out, and yet no one can say where the yellow ceases or where the red begins. No lines of demarcation can be traced between the purple and the pink ; between the orange and the green ; and there are three long miles of this chromatic glory. Three miles of gorgeous color and of fantastic forms. Then, beyond, a score of miles of shadow and solemnity.

Yes, as we turn and look in another direction we see the somber pine-clad walls between which the river there flows on for twenty miles, walls not less high nor less imposing

than those immediately below the falls, walls which, despite
the absence of all color save a deep, rich green, possess a
grand, stern beauty of their own.   That misty, shadowy
nave is, in the eyes of many, as beautiful as the brilliant
chasm from which we have turned away.   The pine-trees,
of which unnumbered millions are stationed in the park, are
crowded in multitudes at the canon's brink, as if in eagerness
to look upon the scene.   Some, like the more courageous
soldiers of a hesitating army, have already dared to clamber
down the walls ; while others — veritable heroes these —
have reached the very border of the stream itself.

Let us now turn back and wander through the forest,
where we shall see the glory of sunset stealing between the

Photograph by F. Jay Haynes, St. Paul

FROM INSPIRATION POINT

CONVERGING SLIDES

tall straight trunks to gild the cañon walls beyond. Every
evening, returning from the contemplation of the cañon, it
was through these beautiful forest-scenes that our path led
us. Often the skies flamed with gold and yellow. At other
times, the background against which the trees were silhouetted
was of brilliant red, pale pink, or tender green. It seemed
as if there in the west the gods were preparing the gorgeous
colors with which, during the long, still night, they would re-
touch the frescos on the cañon walls.

Most travelers are content to view the cañon from the
points to which I have already led you. Others remain
unsatisfied until they have looked into the great chasm from
"Artists' Point," the one perfect point of view, which is
unfortunately on the other bank, and in 1896 was well-nigh
inaccessible. There was no bridge; the crossing of the river
below the falls was utterly out of the question; but there
remained the possibility of crossing far above the upper

gorge, where the waters, although swift-flowing, present a
level, navigable surface. But there has not been a boat
upon the river since the last one, very fortunately empty,
was swept away and dashed to pieces by the cataracts.
No boat! No bridge! The river being now too deep and
swift to ford, I turn in my difficulty to the gallant soldiers
of Uncle Sam, who are stationed at the cañon. The ser-
geant in command at the little military camp enthusiastically
comes to my assistance, and at sunrise next morning I find
him a little way above the rapids, slowly poling upstream
a raft, which he has built expressly for our excursion. At
last we reach a point from which he deems it safe to put
out into the current, where the waters, swift as those of a

STUPENDOUS DETAILS

mill-race, are gliding on in their eagerness to plunge into the yawning cañon, just one mile beyond. There was, of course, no actual danger, yet the thought was ever present that our raft, if left to its own devices, would at

ABOVE THE FALLS

OUR FERRY

A MILITARY GUIDE

Photograph by F. Jay Haynes, St. Paul

THE GREAT FALLS FROM BELOW

once follow unresistingly that treacherous flood, bound through the rapids and plunge over the first fall, then dash through the upper cañon, and finally meet annihilation in the whirlpool at the bottom of the great cataract.

EXCHANGING SIGNALS

In safety, however, we arrive upon the farther shore. Then we skirt the right bank through a thick growth of pine, and while we are walking through the forest, thunder-showers come and go with great frequency and fury. We are soon drenched to the skin, but pressing on we reach the edge of the forest; the earth appears to open at our feet, and the cañon yawns

DRIFTING VAPORS

before us, deep and mysterious.   Vapors are surging upward
from its depths, but fortunately the sun is beginning to break
through the clouds above.   A shaft of sunshine touches a
portion of the opposing wall, and another brilliantly illumi-
nates the pinnacles of white and gold, while others chase the
vapors rapidly away.   The fears that rain and fog will render

Photograph by F. Jay Haynes, St. Paul
THE CAÑON OF THE YELLOWSTONE FROM GRAND VIEW

our excursion fruitless are dispelled, as, reaching another
point of view, we exchange salutes with friends on the other
rim.   We shout to them, they shout to us ; but the sounds
meet only half-way and then fall into the depths between.
We cannot hear, nor are we ourselves heard.   The river's
rumbling mocks our puny efforts to span the deep chasm with

a bridge of vocal sound.   We must attempt to span it with
our gaze.   Few of the great sights of this world have power
to thrill us more than this vista of the cañon of the Yellowstone.   We are unable to tell what most impresses us : the
immensity of the great gulf, the infinite glory of its colored
walls, the struggling river far below, the stately army of tall
pines massed on the brink and pressing forward, apparently
as eager as we to drink in all the splendor of the scene.

UPSTREAM FROM ARTISTS' POINT

All these things go to compose the scene, to form that
indefinable majesty that inspires us — to hold our peace.
Silence is the only eloquence that can avail us here.   No
man has yet found language to express the majesty of this
abyss of color.   But, we ask, will no voice ever perfectly express in words what we all feel but dare not, cannot speak ?
Will no great poet of the new world, inspired by these
grandeurs, ever utter the immortal song in which our vaguest
thoughts shall find interpretation ?   Great, great indeed must

be the soul of him who would give adequate expression to the reverential awe inspired by a scene like this.

But what is man that he should strive to utter the unutterable? The emotions that overwhelm us here can be expressed only in one language, and that is not a mortal language ; it is the language of those to whom all mysteries have been revealed — the great eternal, wordless language of the soul : a language that we may not understand until the gates of death have closed behind us.

THE CAÑON OF THE YELLOWSTONE FROM ARTISTS' POINT

THE GRAND CAÑON OF ARIZONA

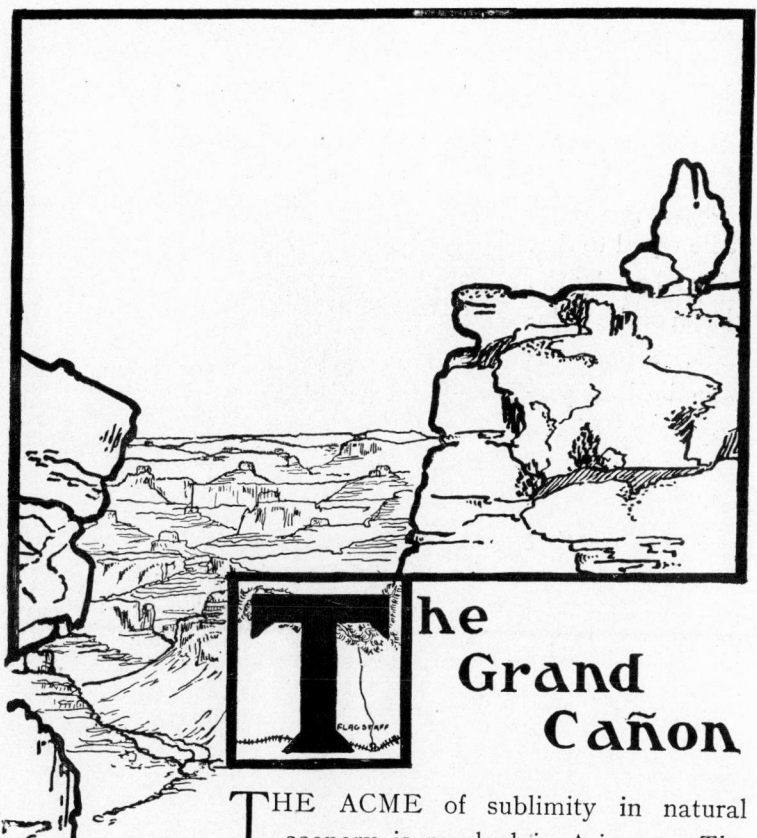

The Grand Cañon

THE ACME of sublimity in natural
scenery is reached in Arizona. The
world is not aware that this is true, nor do I hope to prove
that it is true except to those who, with an interest aroused
by words that are inadequate and pictures that fall far short of
the reality, shall some day undertake the marvelous journey
that glorified for me the summer of 1898.

The cañon of the Colorado River has become for me a
haunting memory, dwarfing all things that I have seen,
belittling all the gorges, all the mountains that in the past
impressed me, robbing the sun of Africa of its luster, causing

the colors of the Orient to fade.　I have
to-day a new and totally different standard by which to measure all that I
intend to see before the greater,
the eternal journey is begun ; and
I am certain that in this life
there is awaiting
me no other spec-
tacle equal to that
afforded by the
chasm of the Colo-
rado.　It has revo-
lutionized my per-
ceptions of the
beautiful and the
sublime.

I believe that
when we behold
that scene for the
first time, a series
of new brain-cells
is generated, and
until they have be-

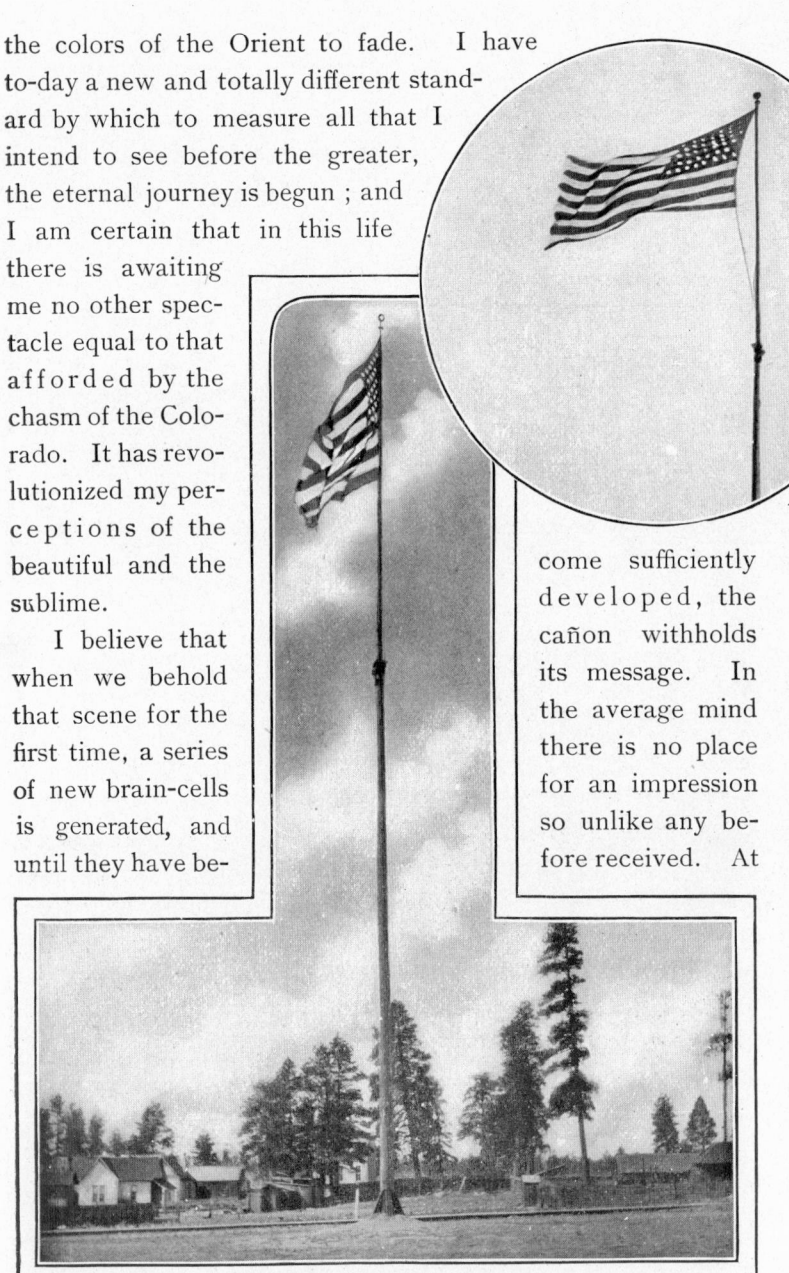

THE FLAG

come sufficiently
developed, the
cañon withholds
its message.　In
the average mind
there is no place
for an impression
so unlike any be-
fore received.　At

Photograph by Mary V. Worstell

THE FLAGSTAFF OF FLAGSTAFF

first sight the mentality is dazzled.   He who looks but once
sees not the cañon.   He who would know its glory must first
prepare the tablets of his mind,—erase all preconceived im-
ages, and then with reverence approach the brink, and sitting
there day after day teach his blind eyes and blinder sense to
read through the medium of feeling the exalted message which
this supremest of earthly scenes imprints upon the soul.

And every time we read the story changes ; it is never
twice the same and it becomes ever more glorious at each
perusal, until those who have learned to read its message
tremble at thought of grander chapters and long for their former ignorance that they may recommence ere they approach
a climax too overwhelming to be borne by the human mind.

FLAGSTAFF, ARIZONA

And having said so much in praise of that which is to be my theme, I must not fail to offer here and now apologies for the unsatisfying treatment to which this theme must of necessity be subjected. Yet why should I apologize? It is not in the power of man to put in words the glory of the cañon. Many have tried and all have failed, as I shall fail; there are degrees of failure that is all. Art has attempted to portray what tongue has not been able to translate, and art has failed. I say it boldly: No painting, photograph, or sketch can do more than suggest to those who have not seen. Photographers by scores have risked their lives to reach that one elusive point of view where the grand lines of majesty would meet one another at the focal plane, but all have failed.

But though all pho-
tographic records are
failures, knowing them
for failures, you
can at least
consider

SALOONS

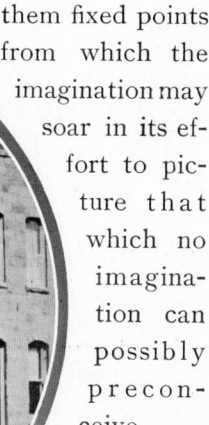

THE HOTEL

them fixed points from which the imagination may soar in its effort to picture that which no imagination can possibly preconceive.

To reach this greatest scenic marvel of the world, there is but one route practicable for ordinary travelers ; only the south side of the cañon is accessible to those who have not the months of leisure and the untold energy required for the exploration of the almost unknown land that stretches away upon the north into Utah. Accordingly, being neither explorers, geologists, nor trappers, we chose the easiest, most rapid, and most attractive route. By rail we have been whisked across the fertile state of Kansas, across the southeast corner of clear-aired Colorado into New Mexico, past the quaint old town of Santa Fé, the second oldest city in our country, where civilization had taken root even before the Pilgrims landed, past the stations where some day we hope to turn aside to visit the Indian pueblos of Acoma and Zuñi, the petrified forests and the famous Mesa Encantada, or Enchanted Mesa, so recently the cause of scientific controversy. But all these things, intensely interesting as they are, must wait another visit. Even the Snake Dance of the Moki

Indians cannot now arrest us. With the Grand Cañon on our minds, all other things seem for the present petty. Accordingly our train flies on across the desert and the wooded lands of Arizona toward the San Francisco Mountains. They rise from a plateau itself eight thousand feet above the sea ; their summits pierce the clouds five thousand feet above the general level of this great tableland, a province in itself. They are the guide-posts which warn the traveler to alter his course from west to north, and change his railway coach for a four-horse stage, for at the base of San Francisco Mountains lies the town of Flagstaff, Arizona, the starting-point for the stage ride to the cañon.

The arrival of our party with cameras and chronomatographs, with almost a mile of film, and rather more than two hundred weight of plates, causes the citizens to smile and

ON THE MAIN STREET

IN THE FOREST

murmur to themselves, "Here comes another group of san-guine photographers, doomed to disaster and defeat."

Flagstaff has been very aptly described as a nice little town with nothing Puritanical about it ; nor is it hypocritical. For barefaced honest badness, all on the surface, commend me to this frank and open town of Flagstaff, Arizona.   We

ABANDONED CLIFF DWELLINGS IN WALNUT CAÑON

first pass three saloons, then a restaurant, a newstand, and a barber-shop, and then another group of drinking-halls.   And there are no screen doors to hide the bars, and no attempt is made to persuade the passing visitor that the men who sit behind the numerous green tables, toying with piles of silver dollars, are money-changers or collectors of the revenue. Nor are the men who sit in silent circles around the smaller

Photograph by Sumner W. Matteson

CLIFF HABITATIONS IN WALNUT CAÑON

tables, playing solitaire. No; gambling is not winked at by the municipality, it is boldly smiled upon, and flourishes like a green bay-tree upon a score of green baize tables. Even the smoking-room of our hotel nightly resounds to the click of the ivory chips along with the chink of silver dollars; but in the glorious, healthful atmosphere of Arizona much of the abjectness of these pitiable pursuits is lost.

Having an afternoon at our disposal we seize the opportunity for visiting the curious cliff-dwellings about eight miles away in Walnut Cañon. What people dwelt in these rude semi-natural shelters, why they dwelt there, and when, are questions that have not been answered; but it is probable that the inhabitants were of the same race as the Pueblo Indians of the Southwest, and that they used these hidden homes as places of abode during periods of warfare or invasion.   To-day they are deserted; the bits of broken pottery, which are occasionally picked up by the wondering stranger, are all that tell of a past human presence here. This cañon must have been indeed a safe retreat.   Although several hundred feet in depth, its presence is entirely unsuspected until we find ourselves upon its brink; for all round about, a lovely forest clothes the level surface of the earth, inviting us, new-comers from the world of cities, to linger and renew acquaintance with Nature.   And Nature has to-day put on here a robe of spring.   The eternal fascination of young June is in the atmosphere; here we bid farewell to the grimy world that we have left behind us,

SUBURBS OF FLAGSTAFF

and try to attune our souls to the concert-pitch of nature, that they may vibrate in faultless, unbroken harmony with the supreme impressions that are soon to strike upon them; for with our eyes we are to see a symphony of form and color,

Photograph by Sumner W. Matteson
IN THE COCONINO FOREST

we are to look upon a world of silence, light, and color, that is more eloquent of grandeur than any musical composition that ever stirred the soul of man.

Returning to Flagstaff, we make our final preparations, reducing our luggage to its lightest littleness, and bright and early on the following morning drive briskly away casting a backward glance at the old flag that floats from the tall pole from which the town takes its name. Alas! this splendid flagstaff, the tallest and finest we have ever seen, save one at the World's Fair, is doomed to quick annihilation; for ere we return from our long drive it was completely shattered by a thunderbolt. We found it a week later a mere stump, its middle lengths lying round about like riven logs, its upper shaft scattered in a million tiny chips far and wide, as if a storm of shavings had overwhelmed the town. But it will be soon replaced, for there is here no lack of towering trees from which to form flag-poles and masts for ships. ''What, are there trees in Arizona?'' we asked incredulously, when a companion in the train referred to a friend in Flagstaff, who had made a fortune in the lumber business. One of the noblest forests in America adorns these Arizona highlands, and our route to the cañon lies for fifty miles or more through an open park-like country, where splendid pines, piñons, and cedars stand like a multitude of kings; and they seem conscious of their dignity, since they stand each at a respectful distance from the others. For a few miles out from Flagstaff, fences accompany and guide us; like a long line of outriders these barriers of rails escort us, until at last, seeing us fairly started on the proper trail to

SIX-IN-HAND

COACH AND TRAILER

the Grand Cañon, they halt suddenly and leave us to drive on
without their guidance across these noble parks of open
woodland, the gathering-places of uncounted forest monarchs.

All this is very different from what we have expected to
find in Arizona.   We pictured this drive as a weary progress
across a sage-brush desert.   How grateful are we to find it
a delightful dash over pine-needles and across cool shadows
cast by arborescent sunshades.   And this surprise is but the
first and least astounding that is to greet us in this unfamiliar,
unappreciated, misrepresented Territory.   I wish that I
could put in words the sweet exhilaration that comes with
every breath of this dry, cool air through which we ride,
perched high on the box-seat behind six toiling horses.

Here, as in the Yellow-
stone, it is a joy to feel
oneself alive.   We travel
thus for one day, ten or
eleven hours long, the distance covered being al-
most seventy miles.   Four
relays of six horses each
enable us to make fast
time, and save the jour-
ney from being a weary

FROM THE FRONT SEAT OF THE TRAILER

one, as it would be were we compelled to use one team for the
entire drive.   When there are so many passengers that one
coach would be overcrowded, a second coach or "trailer" is
attached, transforming our conveyance into a long train that
measures forty-eight feet from the tips of the leaders' noses
to the tail-board of the trailer.   Unhappy are the mortals who
become inmates of that trailer ; they assiduously collect all the
dust, their view is cut off by the forward coach, and they see
little else.   When crossing the broad stretch of desert that

Photograph by H. C. Vroman, Pasadena

THE SAN FRANCISCO MOUNTAINS

separates the two delightful timber regions, deep wheel-ruts
in the yellow soil cause the first coach to act like an over-
laden schooner in a heavy sea : a nerve-shaking inclination
to starboard is followed by a sudden reeling lurch to port,
accompanied by suppressed exclamations, and frantic clutch-
ings at the stanchions.   These antics of our flag-ship are
seen by those in the trailer through a cloud of dust, and
serve as prophecies and warnings that they may know just
what their craft is going to do, and be prepared to hold tight

9

at the proper moment.   These little vagaries, however, serve
to relieve the monotony of this stage of the journey, and to
increase the appetites with which we soon attack a wholesome luncheon at a half-way station, called "The Cedars."

Throughout the day the San Francisco Mountains have
been ever-present features of the view.   They are extinct
volcanoes, and are among the grandest volcanic piles in the
United States.   Snow lies upon their summits nearly all the

Photograph by the Detroit Photographic Company
HALF-WAY HOUSE AT THE CEDARS

year, for no fires are now there to melt their icy caps.   And
near at hand are uncounted volcanic cinder cones, rising like
gigantic ant-hills from the level floor of the plateau.   We see
them sharply defined against the sky as we scan this, the
only blank page of our journey—a dull brown page that lies
between the verdant leaves on which the pictures of the
Arizona forest are printed in deep green.

Far to the right we may discern the pale pink tones of the
far-off "Painted Desert," beyond which lies the country of

THE SAN FRANCISCO MOUNTAINS

Photograph by the Detroit Photographic Company

VOLCANIC CINDER CONES

the Mokis,—a country to which we are soon to make our way, for there is in the west no region richer in color and barbaric strangeness than that desert home of the little Moki nation.

Erelong these barren miles are covered, and once more the forest closes in around us ; the ghostly aspens, with their quaking leaves and gleaming bodies, adding an uncanny note to the rich gloom of the forest depths.   But all this time there is no hint of cañons, no thought of heights or depths, not a suggestion of sublimity.   Beauty and exhilaration, the curious and the interesting, have char-

acterized the day's experiences, but nothing has yet thrilled us.   We have been happy, but we have not been impressed, until—late in the afternoon — we glance toward the northeast and see re- vealed, but oh, so faintly, in far-off re- gions, whether of sky or earth we cannot yet be sure, a vision of rosy glory, a suggestion of the

ASPENS

infinite, a something that takes hold on the attention and will not let it go ; a something that in spite of all its vague- ness, remoteness, and unearthliness, causes our pulses to beat faster, for we know that yonder pinkish line is an emanation of the glory of the cañon, brooding on the dis- tant farther shore of the great gulf that we have come so

PARK-LIKE VISTAS

far to see.   It is soon lost to view ; our weary horses now attack the last ascending mile of the long trail and seem to travel with exasperating slowness, since our thoughts outspeed them in our haste to be upon the cañon brink and to know at last the true meaning of those words so often misapplied, ''sublime'' and ''beautiful.''

"THE CAÑON EXPRESS"

Another mile and we are near our destination, although no further sign of anything aside from sylvan scenery is manifest. And even when at last the tents of the Grand Cañon Camp loom snow-white amid the trees, we feel that there is some mistake; the cañon cannot be so near, and its grand presence so utterly dissembled.

NEARING THE CAÑON

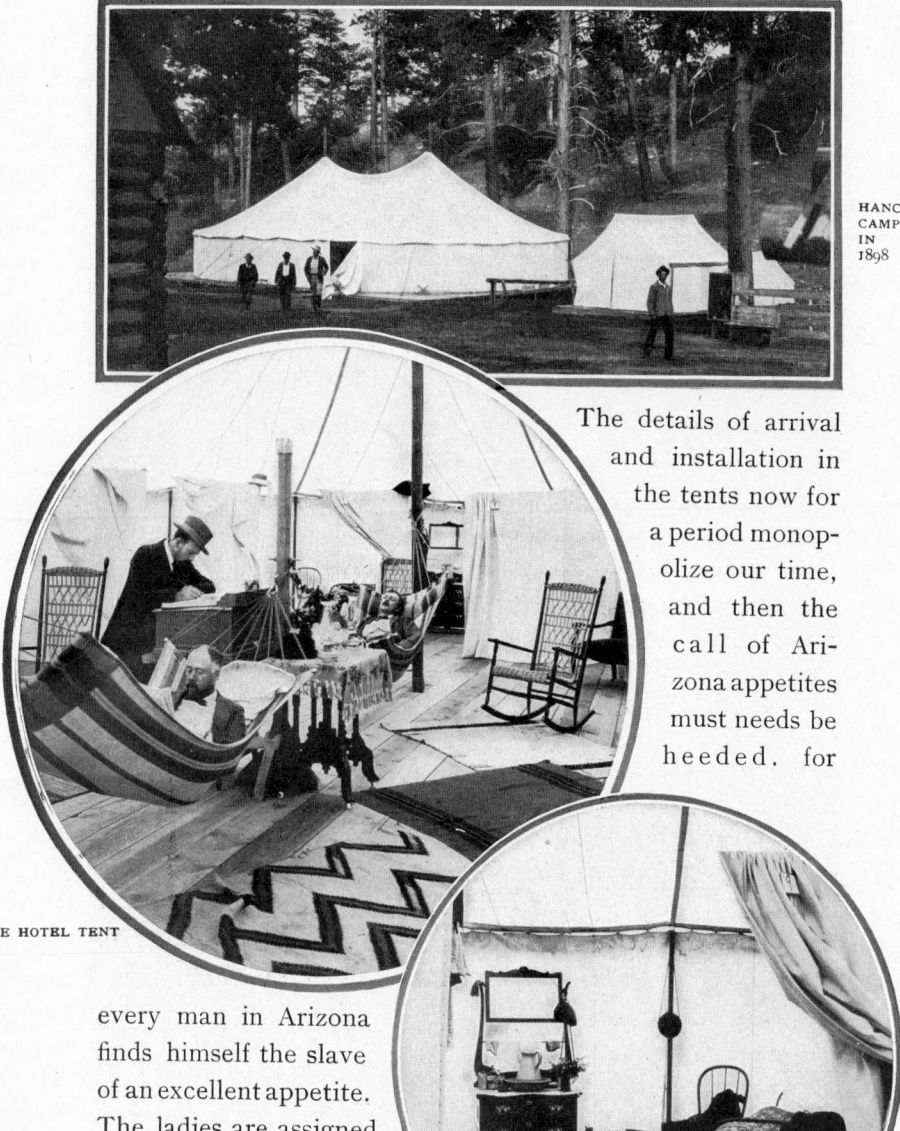

HANCE'S
CAMP
IN
1898

THE HOTEL TENT

ROOM NUMBER NINE

The details of arrival and installation in the tents now for a period monopolize our time, and then the call of Arizona appetites must needs be heeded, for every man in Arizona finds himself the slave of an excellent appetite. The ladies are assigned to single tents, of which a score are scattered about. The men, all hungry as wild beasts, are led into a canvas caravansary big as a circus tent, where canvas cages for each one of us have been provided. We write our names in the register of this unique hotel, and then pick up and curiously peruse another volume of hand-writing, marked, "John Hance's Visitors' Book." In it we find set down impressions of the cañon writ by men and women of all nationalities, all ages, and all grades of culture ; and from that library of eloquence let me quote.

To begin with, our attention is focused on the, as yet unknown, personality of Captain John Hance, the owner of the book, by this entry : "John Hance is one half — the Cañon is the other half." This instantly inspires a desire to meet the cañon's other half and when a moment later that desire is fulfilled, we gaze with awe on Captain Hance and call to mind a second statement found in the Cañon Bible : "God made the Cañon. John Hance made the trails. Without

AT HANCE'S

Photograph by the Detroit Photographic Company
CAPTAIN JOHN HANCE

the other, neither would be complete.'' I leave it to theo-
logians to tell just what the author meant — whether the
incompleteness was an attribute of Hance or of the Deity.
The author of this line was, by the way, a man well known
in Arizona as the best sheriff that ever captured outlaws in
the territory ; Bucky O'Neill, who died, as he had lived, like
a hero, among the Roosevelt Rough Riders on the hill of
San Juan at Santiago.

But as we sit on the veranda of the Log House, which is
the nucleus of the camp, let us cull a few more gems of eloquence from Hance's book of gold, and thereby fit our minds
for the enjoyment of the cañon. A would-be poet writes : —

"Almighty Jove, thy wondrous hand
Hath carved with skill this Cañon Grand.''

The next man writes :   '' The Cañon is the boss ditch of the
world.''   And farther on, appended to a detailed description

of a ride along the rim, some gushing girl has added this post scriptum : —

"P. S.—I think that it is very deep and grand and that it must have taken a very long time to make it. I would like to stay here forever, it is so beautiful."

Then comes the bold hand of a man, but not a very old one, for he writes: "I fully agree with the above, and desire to record the statement that a pleasant lady adds much to the enjoyment of the trip."

But why do you not lead us to the brink and show us that which we have come half-way across the continent to see? Why linger in this little camp concealed amid the trees when there awaits us so superb a spectacle? Why do you hesitate? Because I fear to disappoint you. I fear that I shall not be happy in the choice of the words with which to usher you into the presence of that scene. I am afraid that the only pictures that I can show you will not produce

THE CAMP FROM THE RIM

WHERE THE TRAIL BEGINS

upon you the impressions that they should. I fear that you will misjudge both the cañon and also him who seeks to show it you, because of the imperfect media of revelation. A soul returned from Paradise would scarcely be at a greater loss for words or similes than one who strives to give the message of the Colorado Cañon to an expectant audience. And yet it must be done, no matter how ill.

Let me then beg your sympathy and pray your pardon while I slowly draw the veil, and with reverential gesture reveal at first a mere glimpse, and then another until at last the mind and eye be prepared to take

ON THE RIM

and hold impressions born of wider vistas, which in themselves are but puny fractions of a mighty entirety that cannot be revealed.   Within half a hundred yards of our
forest-hidden tents yawns this unworldly chasm ; great rocks
stand about trembling on the brink, old pine-trees shed

AYER'S PEAK

their cones into these hazy depths that are not fathomable
to the eye.   And we, unless we are of sterner stuff than
the insensate rocks, must tremble too as we stand here
listening to the most appalling silence that ever smote the
ear of man, an awful silence that seems to tell the endless
story of eternity and death.   The sensation of him who for
the first time looks and listens is one of expectant suspense.

We gaze and wait and wait ; for surely something is about to happen. This cannot last ; it is not possible that a scene like this can remain unchanged ; it cannot be that it is immobile ; surely it must soon move or change. This rock must fall, these walls be shaken by an earthquake, or yonder cliff that soars above us must surely become animate and bow its proud head in reverence to the glory that is in the earth beneath and in the sky above. And yet the seconds

Photograph by the Detroit Photographic Company
A POINT OF VANTAGE

and the minutes pass, and in all the earth there is no sound, no movement, and no change, unless we count the involuntary gasp with which we greet each wider vista, the pounding of our hearts, and the epoch-making change that is occurring in our minds — the shattering of old ideals of beauty and of grandeur, the forming of a new standard by which in the future we shall measure all that is beautiful or grand. And still, what we have yet seen is as nothing — mere

A CAÑON CLIFF

glimpses of infinity, mere peeps at things which in the great ensemble of the cañon will never more be recognized or noted.

The towering cliff on which we take our stand a moment later appears like the supremest point, the summit of this Cañon World ; and yet it is a tiny nothing, a mere crinkle in the wall, completely lost to view, like a thousand of its equals, when from a point below we strive next day to locate and to recognize it. For want of a more striking and a newer simile, we must liken the man who, balanced there aloft, looks down upon us, to an insect ; but though a man perched on these pinnacles looks small and puny, he cannot feel his littleness. At least, no man of soul can here feel insignificant ; the fact that his mentality is big enough to see and feel that which is here revealed makes every thinking man appear respectable in his own eyes, and makes the poet or the dreamer feel himself akin to the immortals. I hold that no well-balanced mind finds itself petty

A RIVER-CHANNEL ONE MILE DEEP

in the presence of the cañon.   It is proud to possess perceptions of grandeur equal to the task imposed upon them.
There is an exaltation in the thought that the human consciousness is able to conceive a sense of such grandeur, and to
find enjoyment in a spectacle so overwhelmingly magnificent.

Photograph by the Detroit Photographic Company   A PA

And as in imagination we stand upon another pinnacle
and let our gaze sweep far and wide across the world of
wonder, let me borrow the words of Captain Dutton, the geologist, whose marvelous descriptions are unfortunately buried
in bulky tomes of Government Reports.   He says that "the
lover of nature, whose perceptions have been trained in the
Alps or in any other mountain region, enters this strange

region with a shock and dwells here for a time with a sense
of oppression and perhaps with horror.   Whatsoever things
he had learned to regard as beautiful and noble, he would
seldom or never see, and whatsoever he might see would
appeal to him as anything but beautiful and noble.   Whatso-

THE CAÑON

ever might be bold and striking would at first seem only
grotesque.   But time brings a gradual change.   He suddenly
becomes conscious that the outlines which at first seemed
harsh and trivial have grace and meaning ; that forms which
seemed grotesque are full of dignity ; that magnitudes which
had added enormity to coarseness have become replete with
strength and even majesty ; that colors which had been

esteemed unrefined, immodest, and glaring, are as expressive, tender, changeful, and capacious of effects as any other.''

And as we change our point of view let me continue in Captain Dutton's words, for he has said these things so well that no one need attempt to say them better : ''The Grand Cañon is a great innovation in modern ideas of scenery, and in our conceptions of the grandeur, beauty, and power of nature. As with all great innovations, it is not to be comprehended in a day or a week nor even in a month.

''Great innovations, whether in art or literature, in science or in nature, seldom take the world by storm ; they must be understood before they can be estimated, and must be cultivated before they can be understood.

Photograph by the Detroit Photographic Company

THE CAÑON NEAR PEACH SPRINGS

"It is so with the great cañon. . . . Subjects which disclose their full power, meaning, and beauty as soon as they are presented to the mind, have very little of those qualities to disclose. Moreover, a visitor to the chasm comes with a picture of it created by his own imagination. He reaches the spot, the conjured picture vanishes in an instant, and the place of it must be filled anew. Surely no imagination can construct out of its own material any picture having the remotest resemblance to the Grand Cañon. In all the vast space beneath and around us there is very little upon which the mind can linger restfully.

"It is useless to select special points of contemplation. The instant the attention lays hold of them it is drawn to

Photograph by the Detroit Photographic Company
THE INNER GORGE NEAR PEACH SPRINGS

something else, and if it seeks to recur to them, it cannot
find them.   Everything is superlative, transcending the power
of intelligence to comprehend it.

   " There is no central point or object around which the
other elements are grouped and to which they are tributary.
The grandest objects are merged in a congregation of others
equally grand.   If any one of these stupendous creations had
been planted upon the plains of central Europe, it would
have influenced modern art as profoundly as Fujiyama has
influenced the decorative art of Japan.   Yet here are hundreds of them swallowed up in the confusion of multitude.''

   Must we not envy the unknown beings who in ages past
dwelt in the presence of this scene — in stone houses reared

IMMENSITY!

Photograph by the Detroit Photographic Co.

THE GRAND CAÑON OF THE COLORADO RIVER

upon the summits of these gray columnar towers that rise within a few yards from the rim? Vestiges of dwelling-houses are still visible upon one of the nearest summits, and at many other points within a few miles of our camp. Our first day on the cañon's rim is full of wonder and surprise, a day forever memorable, but not more memorable than the days that are to follow.

It is one form of intense pleasure to view the cañon from above; it is a totally different experience to go down to its very depths and dip our fingers in the murky waters of the Colorado River, that in places glides with oily smoothness, in others foams and fights in its black granite gorge six thousand feet below, so far away that no sound of its struggling reaches us, buried so deep that it scarce seems to bear relationship to the living rivers of the upper world.

To ramble on the brink calls for no effort greater than that attending a stroll along a forest path, for a smooth, safe, and almost level trail has been constructed, winding away and following the shore line of the bays and gulfs, to the tip

ROCK-FRAMED DEPTHS

ends of promontories jutting into space ten miles distant. Each step in advance reveals a new and ever-varying vista, and the return along the same easy trail holds in reserve surprises, new compositions of old views, strange new effects of light and shade, of brilliant sunshine, and of gloomy violet shadow.

One day spent on the rim satisfies some minds. We are inclined to tell ourselves that we have seen all that it is pos-

Photograph by the Detroit Photographic Company
ALONE WITH NATURE

sible to see ; and many, feeling thus, depart the next morning after their arrival. But those who stay are rewarded as no travelers have ever been rewarded elsewhere, and the longer they remain the larger their reward ; for every day brings to the eye new powers, opens to the mind new vistas ; the joy of being here increases day by day, until we verge upon the state of perfect happiness. And oh, the infinite variety of our experiences ! We

DEPARTURE FOR THE DEPTHS

have already strolled with ease and safety along the brow of
countless precipices and looked down into a world that
seems inviolable,— a world to which apparently man must
remain a stranger for all time, and yet we, even we, the city-
dwellers, the inhabitants of regions that are commonplace,
may drop into the depths of this unearthly chasm, and, like
Dante, see strange things, yet live to tell of that which we
have seen ; but alas ! not with Dante's
words of power.   Like Dante,
we begin our wanderings in
an obscure savage wood ;
but unlike Dante we are
mounted — not on the
winged horses of the
Muses, but — on the
mules and the burros
of good old Captain
Hance, who in our case
replaces Virgil as guide.
In early morning Captain

STARTING FOR THE TRAIL

Hance rounds up his stock and brings them saddled to the camp. Our wraps, camera, and blankets are tied on the packs, the men select the beasts to whom their lives are now to be entrusted, and climb into the comfortable western saddles. The only lady in our little band of bold adventurers must bow to the strict rules of Captain Hance and don divided skirts, for the old guide will have no ladies in his train who will not ride astride. He keeps a special skirt on hand for those who do not come provided with the proper costume. The

FOLLOWING THE LEADER

reason for this rule will soon be manifest, for when we reach the cañon brink, we, with a tremor born of surprise and of dizziness, launch our animals into the abyss. Now the path down which we have turned appears impossible. When yesterday we passed the place where it forks downward from the trail along the rim, we scarcely noted it, so

A TICKLISH TRAIL

PREHISTORIC PYRAMIDS

Photograph copyright 1899, by H. G. Peabody, Boston

faint and narrow did it look, so steep that we could not suppose that it was the beginning of the famous highway down
which we were to ride upon the morrow.   The pitch for the
first mile is frightful ; in places it almost surpasses the angle of
repose ; and to our dismayed, unaccustomed minds the inclination apparently increases, as if the cañon wall were slowly toppling inwards, and we anticipate the horror of the moment
when the animals will not be able to retain a footing.   And

FROM SUNSHINE TO SHADOW

this impression that the wall is toppling is strengthened into
conviction by an upward glance, for the dizzy rim, from which
we drop away so suddenly, appears to sway ; its sky-line, by
that curious optical illusion peculiar to things that loom above
us, seems to be continually advancing into space, as if in time
the whole gigantic mass would overwhelm us.   Were it not
for the occasional stretches of comparatively level trail the
suspense would soon become unbearable.   The continued
strain upon the consciousness is increased by the strange,
almost human actions of the animals ; by their slow, careful
placing of the feet, by the jolt that follows every downward

step, by the instant of recovery, at some unprotected "elbow" of the trail where one stirrup dangles in the void, the eye plunges down a thousand feet, and the mind goes running back along life's pathway in a hasty search for those matters that are most insistently calling for repentance.

There may be men who can ride unconcernedly down Hance's trail, but I confess that I am not one of them. My object in descending made it essential that I should live to tell the tale, and therefore, emboldened by the thought of a duty that I owed to prospective auditors, I mustered up sufficient moral courage to dismount and scramble down the steepest and most awful sections of the path on foot ; and it takes more courage to get off and walk, while the only woman in the party remains in the saddle, than it does to face the horror of a fall. I say that I descended sections of the trail on foot. "On foot," however, does not express it, but on heels and toes, on hands

Photograph by the Detroit Photographic Company
HANCE ON HIS TRAIL

ART'S SAKE

and knees, and sometimes in the posture assumed by children when they come bumping down the stairs ; thus did I glissade around "Cape Horn," and past a dozen other places, where neither the mocking laughter of the men nor the more bitter words of sympathy from the brave Amazon could tempt me to forget that my supremest duty was to live to give a lecture on the cañon. Captain Hance expressed it best when he referred to the "lecturer who came down part way like a crab." It is unnecessary to explain why I can show no photographs of the dizzy places I describe. I really had not time to press the button ; but later, when with a confidence born of experience we descend another trail, I promise you glimpses of some places where mental hairs invariably stand on end.

And yet the trails are perfectly secure, no lives have been lost here, few accidents occur ; the traveler is safer in the saddle, and as we soon discovered, the mules knew more of the proper way to scramble down this zigzag chute of shattered rock than we. This conviction once rooted in our minds, fear, like the coward

11

ARRIVAL AT THE RIVER

A VERTICAL MILE OF ROCK

thing it is, will vanish, and we begin to wonder how we could have been concerned about so small a matter as our miserable bodies, while scenes of glory are revealed to us at every turn. When we drink in scenes such as these, the senses are intoxicated; but our sure-footed mules are perfectly sober, and with reassuring deliberation they slip and glide, stumble and jolt, deeper and ever deeper into the chasm of the Colorado. If measured by a tape that follows all its curves and angles, its zigzags and its windings, our path is between eight and nine miles long. The distance from the launching-place for mules, upon the brink, to the launching-place for boats, upon the brink of the raging Colorado, is in a direct line about four miles. The difference in altitude between the river level and the summit of the wall is something greater than a mile, about six thousand feet; in other words, the cañon is fully as deep as Mount Washington is high. The walls appear almost to touch the skies, yet the foreshortening is such that their full majesty is not appreciated from below. From below the nearer cliff looks half as high as the real sky-line above it, but in reality this little palisade from which gigantic boulders have been hurled down, is but a mere detail, an insignificant half-step in the grand stairway of the cañon. That which is near to us, although immense, becomes as nothing when we reach a point whence it can be viewed in its relations to the stupendous whole.

But we cannot realize these magnitudes. As Captain Dutton says: "Not only are we deceived, but we are conscious that we are deceived, and yet we cannot conquer the

Photograph by H. C. Vroman, Pasadena

ON THE BANKS OF THE COLORADO

deception.   Dimensions mean nothing to the senses, and all
that we are conscious of in this respect is a troubled sense of
immensity.''

At last the roar of waters tells us that our ride is nearly
ended, that in four hours we have made our way down to a
level to attain which the Colorado has been laboring for ages
upon ages.   A few rods more and we behold the surging
struggles of the great angry prisoner of the cañon ; and as
we dip our fingers in the murky, coffee-colored tide, we feel

Photograph copyright 1899, by H. G. Peabody, Boston

A STORM IN THE CAÑON

the same thrill that comes to him who for the first time
stands upon a long-desired mountain-top and holds his hands
aloft as if to touch the skies.   Strange mountaineering this,
where men go down to reach their goal and scale steep cliffs
to reach the world of men once more !

But as we look around us, we can scarcely realize that
we are six thousand feet below the level of the surrounding
land.   We are disappointed to find no striking acme here,
as the reward for our fatigue and labor.   The descent and

ascent are in themselves such magnificent experiences that there is no possibility of a satisfying culmination at the journey's end. It is as if we found ourselves in a region of broken, rocky mountains, carved into strange weird shapes, but not of overpowering size. The effect of being in a cañon is here completely lost. The Titanic walls have shrunk backward and also

DINNER IN THE DEPTHS

downward behind the minor buttes and palisades, and we look in vain for the outer limits of the gulf. The true sky-line of the cañon is not visible, though here and there some isolated promontory-tip projects into the ether, like a dot left to mark the place where once the huge escarpment stood.

Our thirst assuaged by draughts of water that is almost mud, filtered between the teeth, we first unpack the animals, indulge in a rude picnic beneath a meager cottonwood, and then, during a long, hot afternoon, we wander round about the camp, scaling low cliffs, in an endeavor to reach some stirring point of view. We clamber over rocks along the river brink, watching the river as it glides heavily around the long, sweeping curves, attacks with a fierce ardor the besetting rocks, and then rushes on from rapids into whirlpools, and out again into a broad smooth channel where for a space, its wrath

COOLING THE CANTEENS

appeased, it slips on silently, preparing for fresh struggles, gathering new strength with which to vanquish other greater obstacles below. At length, weary with the day's excitement, we sup in camp at twilight, and spreading down our sleeping-bags or blankets we are soon ushered into dreamland,—a land far less strange, far less unreal than the mysterious night-enveloped chasm that yawns above us, during our disturbed slumbers, like a moonlit gulf of space.

Photograph copyright 1899, by H. G. Peabody, Boston

AFTER THE STORM

It is not granted to every man to sleep six thousand feet underground, yet this place where we make our bed is one mile farther from the soaring moon than the camp in which we slept the night before. Here in the bottom of the cañon perpetual summer reigns, while on the brink above the seasons come and go, winter whitening the brows of all the palisades, and summer wreathing round the head of every cliff a diadem of leaves and flowers. We do not sleep as soundly as we might; the consciousness of the strange, mighty chamber where we lie disturbs our dreams and the muttering of the

Photograph by the Detroit Photographic Co.

GRAND CAÑON OF THE COLORADO

ASLEEP ON THE COLORADO SANDS

deep-voiced Colo-
rado is in our ears.

At last the dawn comes peeping into our apartment
through a world-wide opening in the roof, and it looks down
upon a group of slumberers smug and ridiculous enough to
make Morning laugh.   And laugh she does, with sunny laughter, and we on waking laugh at one another, and running to
the river make a hasty toilet with cold mud for water and
the Arizona sun for towels.   Then at breakfast we indulge in
ham and bread and beans that grow in cans, and sardines
that never saw the sea, and tinned salmon that never learned
to swim ; anything is good enough for breakfast in this glorious Arizona land.   Even the fact that the paper bags containing salt and sugar had exploded in the packs, and had
mingled their gastronomically uncongenial contents, could
not rob the coffee of its savor nor cause us to reject the
tea.   For loss of appetite I can conceive no surer cure than
an excursion to the cañon.   That which people elsewhere
cannot eat they can and send to Arizona.

Then Captain Hance rounds up the animals, saddles the
horses, packs the mules, and we begin our skyward journey.
The weary way is shortened by the tales of Captain Hance,
who is, as all men know, a vivacious chronicler of the most

Photograph copyright 1899, by H. G. Peabody, Boston
THE CURVING COLORADO

unbelievable events that ever happened.   He is the hero of
more strange adventures than any man alive.   Once he was
hanged for horse-stealing — ''stringed up for mor 'n three
hours, and when they ket me down I kem to in ha 'f an hour.
An', moreover, I did n't steal no horses ; they jest come up
and puts their necks into the noose of the halter I was
a-carryin', and foller'd me.''

As a rough rider Captain Hance has made a record, but
he admits that his attempt to leap a horse across the cañon
was a failure.   '' He giv a fine big jump — but when we was
'bout ha 'f-way over, I seed we could n't make it, so I turned
him back.''

As our sturdy energetic horses attack with a surprising
vigor the steep, rough trail that lifts its windings toward the
world above, the journey is beguiled by recollections of these
wonderful adventures of bold Captain Hance.   His marvelous encounter with a gigantic bear is now a cañon classic.
Chased by the hungry beast, Hance drops his gun and rushes
up a tree ; the bear at first throws stones, then picks up
Hance's rifle and looks it over knowingly ; and finally with
almost human dexterity shoulders the Winchester and bangs
away three times at his intended victim.   "I do believe,"
says Captain Hance, "that if they'd 'a' been another ket-
ridge in that gun he'd 'a' shot me, sure."   "What followed?"
we inquire breathlessly.   "Oh, bimeby he got tired and
ambled off."   And to our query, "Did he take the gun?"
the Captain, with a forgiving smile, replies :   "Well, no, he
did n't ; you see there was some honor in him."

We made a motion picture of the Captain telling of his
famous experience with a big silver salmon in the river.

PACKING

CAPTAIN JOHN HANCE'S FISH-STORY

The Captain loves to fish; he also loves to doze, and so one day he tied his line to his left leg and settled down upon the river brink to snooze; a big fish took the bait, jerked slumbering Hance into the flood, and towed him rapidly down stream. "I didn't mind the rapids or the rocks," the Captain tells us; "but I was afeard that when that darn old fish came to a deep whirlpool, he'd sink down to rest in quiet waters at the bottom, and I knew the line wa'n't long enough to let me stay on top. And that's just what he done, pulling me down after him. Of course I didn't want to lose my line, so, seeing there was no other way, I clim down that line hand-over-hand till I reached Mr. Salmon. I whips out my knife, cuts off the line right by his mouth, and giving him a big kick square in the face, I swum ashore, and I never see that fish again."

In early afternoon we reach the forest and pass the morrow restfully in wandering through it, following the old Moki Indian trail, or making excursions

to new points of van-
tage on the rim or to
the far extremities of
capes and promon-
tories whence other
splendid vistas are re-
vealed. The sublime
points of view are al-
most numberless, and
the wandering stran-
ger will every now
and then stumble into
the presence of the
cañon, and with every
new glimpse of the
chasm there is born
a new suggestion of
grandeur, impossible
to translate verbally.

Our journey to
the depths has given
us a new conception

STEEP AS A STAIRWAY

of the cañon. Now that we know its magnitude, we look
upon it with new interest and find that we continually ask
ourselves, How was it made, and when?

The story of the making of the cañon covers a period
not measurable in centuries. Before man was, the cañon
had been; after man shall cease to be, the cañon probably
will continue to exist, and yet the existence of the cañon is
but transitory; its creation, duration, and disappearance are
but incidents in the history of our globe. The surface of the
earth is undergoing constant changes, although one change
may take more centuries than are counted in the life of the
human race. Where land once was, there is now water,

where water is, there will in time be land. So it has been
and will be with this Grand Cañon region.

But let us turn our gaze away from the abyss and look out
upon the forest-covered land that stretches away in simple,
dignified immensity toward east and south. This, probably,
was the aspect of the region before the Colorado carved its
trench and laid bare those layers of colored rock, which had
been deposited here in the long ages during which this dis-
trict was submerged. Geologists tell us that it once formed
the bed of a great arm of the ocean, later that of a brackish
estuary, and later still the bed of a fresh-water lake ; for as
the ages passed, the entire region slowly rose, pressed
upward by some mysterious internal force. It was raised no
less than eighteen thousand feet. It is now only eight thousand feet above the sea, for as it rose, the upper strata, to a

ON THE OLD MOKI TRAIL

thickness of ten
thousand feet,
were planed down
evenly and swept
away, carried off
to another part of
the world by the
all-transporting
waters. Then as
the land, com-
posed of many
colored strata,
continued to be
thrust up, the cli-
mate which had
been damp grew
arid, the waters
decreased in vol-
ume, and became

A GLIMPSE OF THE INNER GORGE FROM THE RIM

Photograph copyright 1899, by H. G. Peabody, Boston
ON GRAND VIEW POINT

unequal to the task of planing down all of the vast area. But the lake remained, fed by the streams that rolled down from the high mountain-regions in the distant north. And its waters began to carve a channel of escape from their arid prison; thus the cañon of the Colorado had its birth. The waters, armed with such tools as sediment and sand and grit, began to file a groove in the slowly uplifting mass of the plateau, and keeping at their work for centuries of centuries, they applied their instruments firmly against the upward moving rocks, and cut and cut, holding their right of way at its old level, while on either side, in the succeeding millenniums, the great walls were rising slowly, imperceptibly. Thus the Colorado did not begin at the top and carve its channel downward for six thousand feet; the land itself has risen, the river has but maintained its former level, filing away for countless ages at its ever-rising bed. And yet the present cañon, deep as it

12

is, does not represent even one half of the work accomplished by the gritty, grinding flood. To appreciate fully the mighty labors of the river, we must in imagination restore the missing upper strata that once were piled above this present surface of the plateau. These missing strata, in the aggregate, were of an average thickness of ten thousand feet; and could we once more spread them out over this denuded table-land upon each side of the Colorado Cañon, the chasm would then appear as an abyss of vastly magnified dimensions, for its vertical depth from the topmost of those vanished layers down to the

GNAWED BY
THE TEETH OF AGES

NATURE'S ARCHITECTURE

FROM A DRAWING BY PROFESSOR W. H. HOLMES

river-bed would be not less than sixteen thousand feet. Had it not been for that even denudation, or planing down, of the entire region during long periods of copious moisture, had the climate become arid a few ages earlier, we should now have an even more stupendous Colorado Cañon, one more than three miles deep.

But the river was not twelve miles wide ; how could it carve so broad a chasm ? We can conceive of this filing process creating a deep narrow cañon two hundred and more miles in length, but that a river, itself less than five hundred feet in width, could have created this vast subterranean mountain region that is from five to twelve miles in width is even incredible. Incredible indeed if we regard the waters as the only agents ; but there are numerous

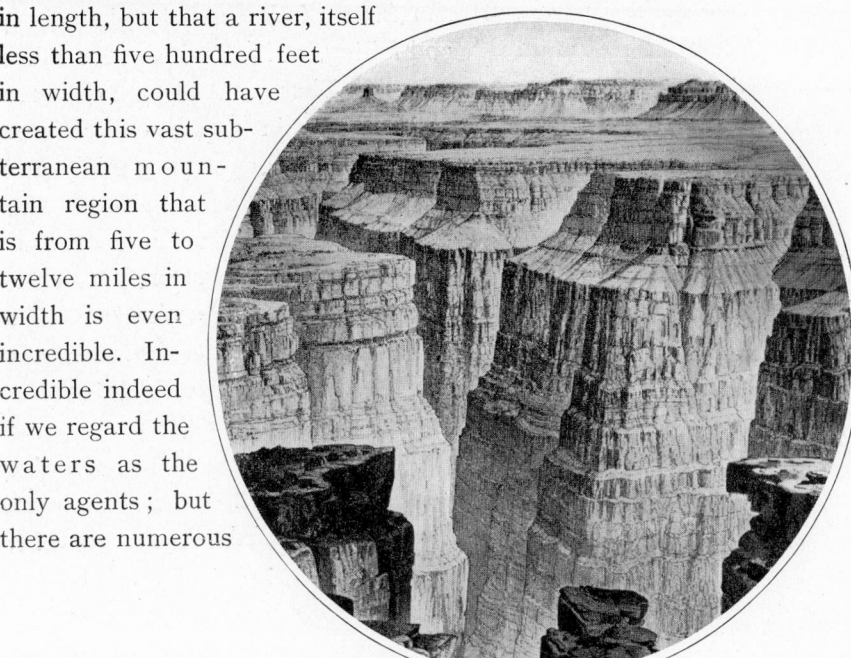

FROM A DRAWING BY PROFESSOR W. H. HOLMES

FROM A DRAWING BY PROFESSOR W. H. HOLMES

other forces that have been ceaselessly at work. The river cuts a trench only as wide as its own water-surface, and no wider. But the cutting of this trench exposes long vertical walls to the action of the elements, which vigorously attack them. The rains fall, the winds blow, frost freezes and sunshine thaws ; the rain-born rills begin to eat into the walls ; they gather sand and sediment and thus as they descend, their force is multiplied, and they erode more and more vigorously. Small fragments of rock are broken from the calm faces of the cliffs by alternating blows of heat and cold, and falling, strike and shatter other fragments from the lower wall. Thus gradually the cliffs are weathered away and slowly recede in opposite directions. In some places the destroying agents work more rapidly and carve out bays and gulfs or narrow gorges and side cañons, thus multiplying the surfaces exposed to attack and denudation. The material torn from the walls by storm-born cataracts, or hurled into the depths by the action of other elements is eventually disintegrated and reaches the river-bank in the form of sand or grit or pebbles. Then the busy river seizes upon it and presses it into service for the prosecution of the endless task of filing down the granite channel, and, thus borne seaward by the hideous earth-laden river, each grain of sand washed down from the proud cliffs, each atom

LOOKING TOWARD THE CAÑON ACROSS THE PLATEAU

broken by storm from the aspiring pinnacles aloft, each
pebble rolled from the high world above by force of ava-
lanche, is compelled to do its share toward the completion of
this never-to-be-completed enterprise of nature, the making
of the Colorado Cañon. And all the rock and earth that
once filled this abyss, after accomplishing its appointed task

Photograph copyright 1899, by H. G. Peabody, Boston
COLOSSAL DETAILS

of cutting, carving, and sculpturing under the direction of the
Master River, has been transported to the Gulf of California.

Thus in the course of ages the cliffs, like parting monarchs, have slowly backed away from one another, until a
zone of glory five to twelve miles in width now separates
them; and this unearthly zone is peopled by strange, gorgeous forms, the offerings left by the retiring monarchs, as
tokens of their former close relationship,—weird, beautiful,
inimitable objects, the like of which no man has ever seen
before, rock carvings as huge as temples, fantastic buttes as

ALL THIS THE WORK OF THE WATERS

big as mountains, and in the very midst of this titanic Field of the Cloth of Gold there lies in sinuous curves a long chain that once was silvery as the virgin waters of a glacier,—a chain that now is brown and rusty with the wear and toil of ages; for the only thing that is not beautiful in this gay Wonder World is the unhappy Colorado River, its architect and builder.

THE COLORADO RIVER

Photograph by W. H. Jackson

WONDERLAND!

Remembering these facts, we can with a more intelligent appreciation of its meaning again descend into the cañon. We chose this time a different starting-point, a different trail. Two or three miles from the little camp of tents where we made our headquarters during our visit in early June, 1898, we find a cosy comfortable hotel, a big log-house, erected and presided over by Mr. Peter Berry. For a hotel proprietor Mr. Berry was altogether too retiring. We were

EARTH-LADEN WATERS

on the point of leaving the cañon in ignorance of the existence of this place, when, quite by accident, we stumbled upon it during an aimless ramble ; but, once discovered, the attractions of this Grand View Hotel, and the Grand View Trail, at the head of which this hotel stands, proved so convincing that in August, after our return from the Hawaiian Islands, we came a second time to the Grand Cañon, purposely to explore that section of the cañon reached by the Grand View Trail, under the guidance of Mr. Peter Berry.

I cannot say enough in praise of our kind host and of the comforts offered by his log hotel. Here, even in the colder seasons, a long sojourn would be a not uncomfortable experience. There is a cheeriness about the interior, an aspect of solidity and warmth in the stout log walls, and a white-aproned, white-capped European personage, quite worthy of the title, "chef," presiding over the cuisine. For one of those wandering Continental culinary artists had drifted to

BERRY'S GRAND VIEW HOTEL

this distant end of earth in the course of his restless world pilgrimage, and while he lingered near the cañon, all visitors to the Grand View Hotel enjoyed the luxury of Continental cooking,—a luxury that here appears to be ridiculously out of place. Our host is a collector of cañon curiosities ; the office is an incipient museum. His greatest treasure is a jar or *olla*, discovered in a cave in the cañon wall,—a cave so inaccessible that it proved almost impossible to bring forth the *olla* in safety. Unlike Mr. Hance, Berry is a man of few

words, but those
few words are al-
ways to the point.
There is nothing
of romance in the
soul of Peter Ber-
ry ; when he meets
a bear, it is not
the bear that does
the shooting ; and
when he catches
a salmon, Peter
Berry eats the fish;
and as for leaping
horses across the
mighty cañon, he
has not wasted his
time in that peril-
ous attempt, but

AT BERRY'S

has sawed wood and hewed rocks and built the Grand View

A CONTINENTAL CHEF

AN OLLA FOUND IN A CAVE

Trail and made it possible for travelers to reach the river at a point where there is no chance of anti-climax, for this trail winds down into the depths of the black archean inner cañon where we may see the river slowly carving out its pathway in the resisting but ever vanquished granite.

Dreaming of the adventures of the morrow, we sleep that solid, health-giving Arizona sleep; and when we wake and look out from our windows, there, swathed in the pink and violet vapors of the morning, is the thing that has been with us in our dreams. The Grand View Hotel is one of the few hotels in the world that bear the title "Grand View" worthily.

But again I must deplore the pitiful inadequacy of the picture-making art. It had been wiser, perhaps, for me to nurse with selfish pleasure my memory of the Grand Cañon rather than to try to make you see in mere pictures the biggest beautiful thing in all the world, the most entrancing scene that ever dawned upon the eye of man. For such it is, and such it will in future be proclaimed by all who look upon it. If I excite your curiosity to see and know, I shall have done enough.

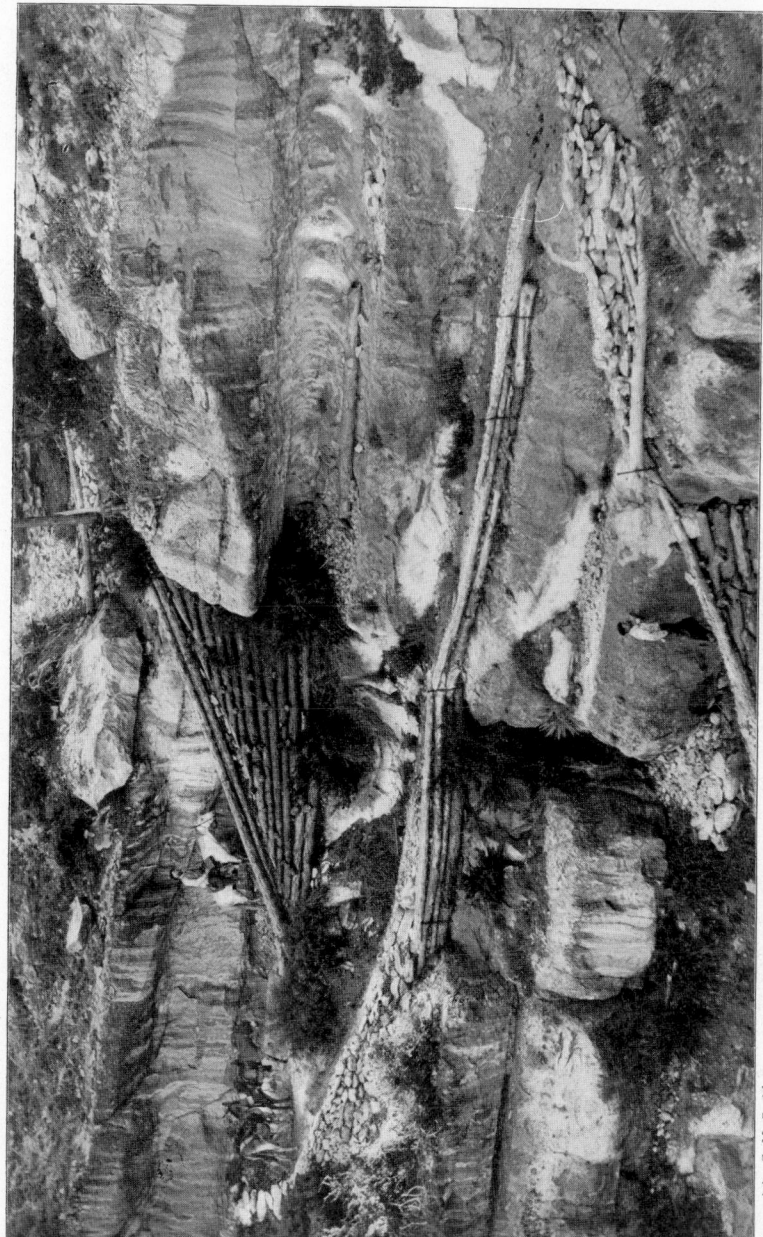

ON THE GRAND VIEW TRAIL

Photograph by G. M. Smith

This time there is no horror in the thought of plunging
into that great sea of beauty, and it is with an eagerness and
an enthusiasm that is unmixed with any fear or hesitancy
that we again push the noses of our horses into space and
begin the all-day journey toward the center of the earth.
From the very first we perceive that the trail makes no
reassuring pretense of gentle inclination ; at once in business-
like fashion it swings downward at most startling angles.

VISTA FROM THE GRAND VIEW HOTEL

The trail, although well constructed and perfectly safe,
is steep enough to be thrilling, nor does it lack short, slippery
turns with precipices underfoot and overhanging cliffs above.
There are enough of these to keep the senses tingling, and to
make the traveler feel as if the horse's reins were connected
with electric batteries, or as if his stomach were asleep.

Knowing the depths to which it must descend within so
limited a time, it wastes no precious minutes in seeking soft
declivities ; instead, it boldly bridges gaps and ravines, or

13

jumps from ledge to ledge, using long slender logs as alpenstocks. The animals at every step start little avalanches down the path, and to the music of the clattering stones we slide and glide with many a sudden stop at corners and many a pirouette at the extremities of every elbow of this zigzag chute. But now and then the trail reposes for a moment on a level ledge, and there the traveler may rest, all save his eyes, for not a moment's respite is granted to the nerves that carry new and grand impressions from the optics to the brain. We see in the course of our descent a replica of almost every scenic marvel of the old world and the new The gorges through which we rode in Corsica, Algeria, or Southern France are reproduced by hundreds, in heroic mold, yet they appear like tiny grooves, scarce worthy our consideration. You have read of the Wonder City of Algeria, Constantine, throned on its mighty citadel of rock, a thousand feet above the Algerian plateau. Here in the cañon there are five hundred imitations of the rocky pedestal of Constantine, and beside any one of them the African original would at

A RESTING-PLACE

AN EASY TURN

once seem a puny boulder.   I could recite a catalogue of
other scenes that would here find their reproductions done
on a scale ten times more grand and more imposing.   But
let us turn to architectural marvels.   We have seen in
Greece and Italy and Sicily the splendid outdoor theaters
of the ancient Greeks and Romans,—theaters with marble
seats for forty thousand people.   Ride with me around
yonder point and let me show you two natural theaters,
twin theaters, a thousand times more ancient than those
of Greece and Rome, ten thousand times more wonderful,
for they were carved by the blind forces of the
earth and not built up with hands; and though
a conception of their magnitude cannot be
conveyed by photographs, the two
could offer seats to the entire

TOWERS AND PYRAMIDS

population of Chicago, and then there would be sufficient
room for half a million more of fashionable late-comers.
And as for the surroundings of America's antique temples

Photograph copyright 1899, by H. G. Peabody, Boston
FROM THE GRAND SCENIC DIVIDE

of the drama, what can Greece, or Italy, or Sicily offer that
is grander and more beautiful than the world of wonder
that here spreads around? Even the far-famed Taormina,
reputed the most lovely place in all the world, can offer to
the spectator in the ruined theater no more lovely vista than
that which greets us as we dizzily swing around yonder cliff
and pause again, not knowing whether to look up or down,
to right or left, for everywhere in earth and sky there is
a something that insistently demands our admiration.

Then, farther down, the trail itself again claims our
attention ; blasé indeed the rider who can come coasting on a

slipping, struggling horse down the long unprotected chute, without reviewing his past life and making New Year's resolutions.   Again the lens fails to convey an accurate impression ; the section of the trail is steeper than it looks.   A man on foot cannot walk down without digging his heels deep into the loose earth and steadying himself by clinging to the rocky walls; and to that wall all timid ones are glued by the horror that rises from the fathomless depths into which a false step, or the slipping of a bit of rock might drop the trembling traveler.   But we made no pictures here until we reached this place next day during the slow ascent.   While coming down, the traveler is too busy making mental snapshots — he has no time to use the camera.   Perhaps you

WALLS AND AMPHITHEATERS

think that I exaggerate the pitch of the path, the sheerness
of the precipice.   If so, glance upward at the ladder down
which we and our struggling beasts have come.   A diagonal
line marks the true pitch — 45 degrees ; there is no need to
tilt the camera to one side to make the picture more effec-
tive.   Yet truth, both verbal and photographic, falls so far
short of giving to one who has not looked upon these scenes a
convincing image of the cañon, that he who is to tell the story
can easily persuade himself that honesty is not the best policy,
that lies are not only pardonable but almost imperative.

By noon our caravan arrives at a crude stone house,
erected to shelter the men who formerly labored in Berry's

copper mines three thousand feet below
the rim.   The mining industry has been
practiced even in the cañon.   In fact,
had it not been for the dis-
covery of this copper mine, the
trail would never have been
built.   The mine has not fulfilled its promise, the cost of
transportation be-
ing great ; but the
trail remains and
will in time become
a source of profit to

FROM THE GRAND VIEW TRAIL

its builders, when
the great tourist
army shall learn
of the new world
to conquer that
awaits them here.
At present, the
accommodation
in these depths is
not luxurious; yet
never did a palace
banquet, served
on golden plate,
taste half so good
as did the patent
soups and canned
meats that were
served in battered
tins on a pine ta-
ble, under ragged

THE STEEPEST STRETCH

awnings.   We all agreed that among the few brief periods of
perfect happiness and contentment that come to a man in life,
we shall be compelled to number the minutes spent here in
satisfying the demands of our vigorous Arizona appetites.

The sleeping accommodations at the mine are not such as
appeal to those who are encumbered with fastidious ideas
concerning snowy linen.   The one virtue of these beds, six
of which graced one room of the shanty, was that they were
well-aired; for they had been airing for at least three months,
ever since the passing of the last caravan of tourists.   These
sleeping-machines were far less comfortable than the bare
ground on which we slept while at the foot of Hance's trail,
but having killed a rattlesnake not half-a-dozen rods away, we
found the exaggerated altitude of our hard couches reassuring.

During the afternoon we made a short excursion to the caves, reached by descending a narrow trail cut in the rock-face of the mesa, and entered by a flat low portal through which our adventurous leader squeezed his way. Within, guided by Peter Berry, we file along low narrow corridors, creep on our hands and knees between half-opened jaws of rock that threaten instantly to close upon us, and then suddenly we stumble into high-arched chambers almost ecclesiastical in architecture. Then, following another corridor, we discover that it ends abruptly at a vertical wall ; but the faint light of the candles reveals a dangling rope, and seizing this we walk with our bodies almost horizontal up the wall, cross to its farther side, and there descend by means of the same rope. We reach at last a point at least one thousand feet from the entrance, and we there turn back, having explored but a fraction of this natural labyrinth ; finally we come in safety to

THE TRAIL AT FORTY-FIVE DEGREES

LOOKING UP A SIDE CAÑON

Photograph copyright 1899, by H. G. Peabody, Boston

the outer world again. We cannot be resigned to wandering in darkness, while above our heads there floats a world
of glory, and while below us yawn almost untraveled depths,
more somber, more inaccessible than those into which we
have already ventured. We are now about two thousand
feet below the miner's hut, about fifteen hundred feet

WRINKLED FACES IN THE ROCK

above the river level. The lower trail, by which we came,
is ruder, rougher, less secure than the upper, but equally
dramatic, and it offers even more thrills of horror to the
mile. The horses were abandoned at a point a few hundred feet above this spot, for we are informed that the trail
thence to the river is possible only for men on foot.

Higher and higher the walls and buttes and pinnacles have risen above us, until the walls of the great black gash that marks the pathway of the river spread downward like two world-wide shadows at our feet. Now, one by one the

A COPPER CAMP IN THE CAÑON

pinkish pinnacles, the rosy towers, and the dull red bastions of the middle cañon, seem to sink behind the darker lower masses, leaving but one or two buttes standing like sentinels to note our downward progress.

Let us creep out around the ledge of rock and peer into that world of somber blackness. At last we see a cañon that agrees with our conception of the word. For until now we have been haunted by the thought that this great outer chasm is not a cañon, that it should have had another and a grander name. The most sublime of cañons that we hitherto have

seen is the many-hued, surpassingly brilliant Cañon of the
Yellowstone, and it is one of the few things in nature that do
not suffer and shrink into utter commonplaceness when measured by the Arizona scenic standard.   In size the Cañon of
the Yellowstone is relatively petty.   This repellent black trench
is deeper by several hundred feet, and it is many times as long
as its northern rival, yet it is only a mere incident in the
greater gulf around it ; it is but a comparatively unimportant
bit of detail still unfinished.   It has a dignity and an impress-
iveness, and when we come to know it, a certain grim and
savage beauty, but it lacks the transcendent loveliness of the
delicately tinted Cañon of the Yellowstone.

    The Cañon of the Yellowstone is to the Inner Gorge of
the Colorado what St. Mark's Basilica at Venice, with its
varied and gorgeous coloring, is to the great rock-temples of
the Nile, with their somber age-worn tones.

    And, moreover, the Yellowstone is alive ; its waters, in-
stinct with life, leap mighty cataracts or gambol playfully in
rapids that are symphonies in
green and white ; while the
Colorado gorge seems to
be dead — its walls are
hung with black, and
its waters creep in
torpor, almost si-
lently save where
they surge and
rattle amid the
murderous rocks
as if in the agony
of death.

    The waters of
the Colorado, when
they give voice, sing

A CAÑON COT

dirges; the waters of the Yellowstone are chanting a perpetual joyous Hallelujah. And as we allow our glance to roam hesitatingly down this dreary channel, there creeps into our minds a picture of four little boats manned by heroic men, being swept onward by the turgid tide from horror to horror, from the unknown into the unknown. Their wonderful voyage was made in 1869. The boats have been for three months in that underworld — they have come from the far north, beyond the place where the Grand River and the Green unite to form the Colorado; the men are the first human beings who have ever dared to venture into what was then a world as full of terror to the moderns as the antipodes were to the men of medieval times. The story of

THE SLEEPING-SHANTY

their voyage is certainly one of the most thrilling and heroic chapters in the annals of American achievement.

The river channel had never been explored. The Indians held that no boat could live in the mad grasp of the river, that rapids everywhere beset the path ; that cataracts high as Niagara hurled the brown flood from one depth to another ; that even if the men should survive the sure annihilation of the boats, there was no pathway to the world that is above ; that should they by long, superhuman effort climb to the upper world, a boundless, trackless, waterless expanse of desert would greet them there. To drift for three long months toward these unknown, but suspected dangers, called for the same grim courage that inspired Christopher Columbus to sail forth into the unknown. Yet for Columbus and his crew retreat was always possible ; for these men there could be no turning back. Uncertainty was on every hand, danger ahead, starvation ever swimming close behind their boats.

ENTERING THE CAVES

Yet brave men were induced to embark upon this seemingly hopeless enterprise by the braver man who led them. That man, who dared this mad ride, who steered his fragile fleet to victory through the dark cañons of the Colorado for more than a thousand miles, was Major John Wesley Powell, of the United States Geological Survey, the hero of our Scientific Army.

The river in places is as calm and tranquil as a well-fed lion, but farther on, where rocks rise to impede its progress, it roars with anger, lashes itself into a fury, and woe betide the helpless craft which then falls into its clutches and becomes the victim of its rage ! Another danger threatens the adventurous craft that trusts itself to the treacherous Colorado. At any moment storms may burst upon the world above — a vast quantity of water be flung into the cañon by a million rills, each adding to the flood its sudden offering, receiving which the Colorado rises fifty feet in about as many minutes. Yet Powell and his men faced all these dangers. They boldly shot the lesser rapids, cautiously crept around the greater, lowering their boats by means of ropes. One boat was lost, with part of the provisions, the others were frequently capsized, frequently threatened with destruction,

IN THE CAVES

UNDERGROUND EXPLORATIONS

and we must not forget that Powell, the leader of this band of heroes had but one arm with which to fight his battle with the waters.

As we stand on the shore of the great river that was conquered by Powell and his little crew, let us record his words written in the depths :

"Our boats go leaping and jumping over waves like herds of deer bounding through forests beset with fallen timber. We recall the warning of an Indian chief, who said in striving to dissuade us — 'Rocks, heap high. Water pony, heap jump. Water catch.

14

OUT FROM THE UNDER-WORLD

'em sure. No see 'em Injin any more. No see 'em squaw any more. No see 'em papoose any more.' Ever before us is an unknown danger heavier than the immediate peril. We camp by night on rocks where there is scarcely room for all to lie, and the discomfort of the night is worse than the toil of the day. Ever watching for rocks, ever listening for obstacles, we are swept on, past cliffs where the soaring eagle is lost to view ere he reaches the summit.'' Then, when one boat containing part of the provisions breaks away while being lowered by ropes over a roaring cataract, he writes, ''It now becomes a race for dinner.''

We cannot blame the three men of that little band, who faltered, finally forsook the expedition, and with their share

AT THE EDGE OF THE GRANITE

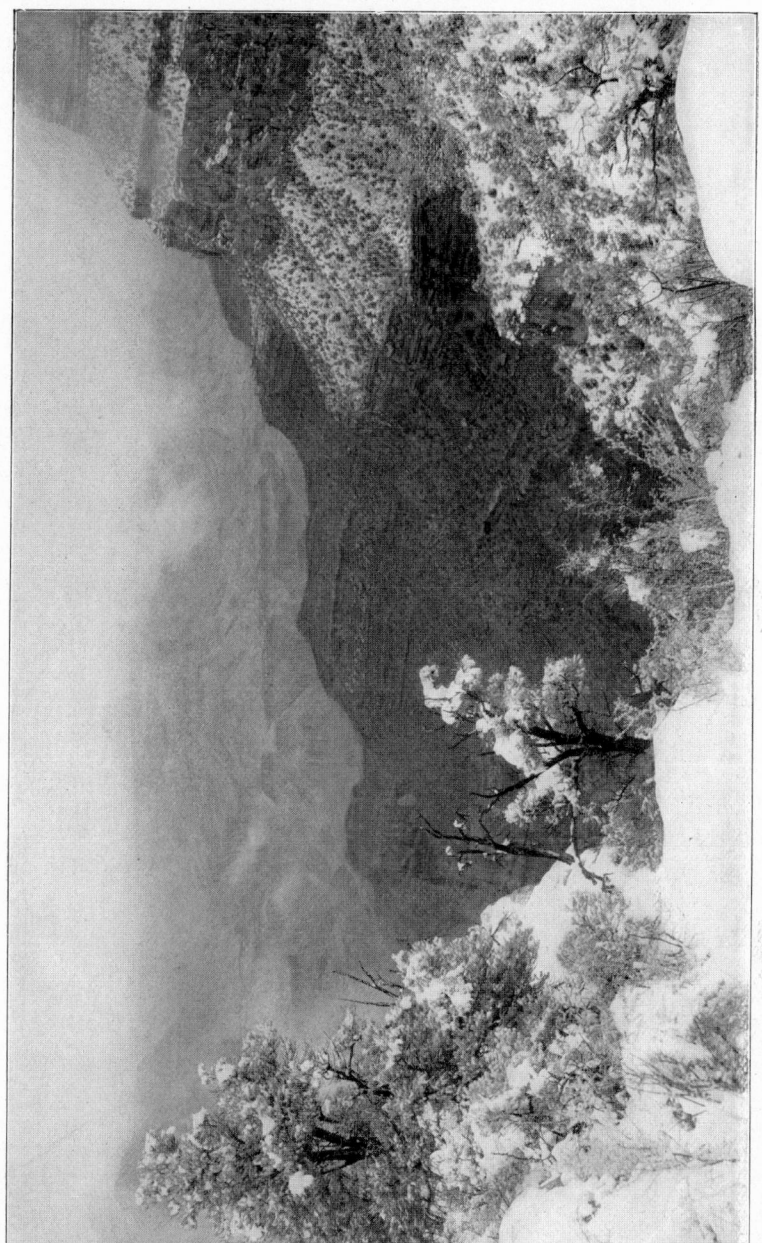

A TOUCH OF WINTER

Photograph copyright 1899, by H. G. Peabody, Boston

Photograph copyright 1899, by H. G. Peabody, Boston

PALISADES

of the provisions started to climb out of the depths which
had inspired them with a fear that could not be suppressed.
We should not
call them cowards
— perhaps more
courage was re-
quired to scale
the then-trailless
cliffs and to face
the waterless and
boundless horror
of the desert up-
on the northern
brink than to re-
main with their
companions in
the boats to meet
the more familiar
horrors of cata-
racts and rapids.

HOT WORK

The river had been merciful to Powell's band; several times it refused to take advantage of their helplessness, as they drifted on with broken oars or capsized boats. The men who trusted to the sullen torrent to deliver them were saved, and lived to give to a wondering, admiring world the first authentic knowledge of the cañon; the three who sought their safety in a perilous ascent of their prison walls and aimless wanderings on the plateau, met with a tragic death, for they were killed by the doubting Indians to whom they told the incredible story of their epic Odyssey.

Remembering this achievement of Major Powell, which in dramatic interest is unsurpassed in the history of American exploration, we marvel at the misconceptions that prevail concerning the Grand Cañon. Well-informed people tell me they have ridden through the Colorado Cañon *while on a railway train*, confusing this chasm with a comparatively petty gorge which lies in the State of Colorado; others are not even aware of the existence of this proudest of all our natural possessions. Children are taught the story of the cañon in the schools of Germany and England, while American men who

MAJOR POWELL'S PATHWAY

Photograph copyright 1899, by H. G. Peabody, Boston

A GRAND CAÑON THOROUGHFARE

Photograph copyright 1899, by H. G. Peabody, Boston

A SIDE CAÑON

THE INNER GORGE OF THE COLORADO

edit journals, and women who read papers in their clubs, ask where the Colorado Cañon is, and are surprised to learn that it is not in Colorado but in Arizona. Even the old Spaniards knew nearly as much about it three hundred and fifty years ago, as do Americans to-day. A company of the conquistadors, seeking the fabled

Seven Cities of Cibola, was eventually led to the brink by
Moki guides and gazed upon this scene as long ago as
1540. This far-away region, whose existence is but now
beginning to be realized by us, was among the earliest por-
tions of America to be explored, and Spaniards sent to Spain
decriptions of this cañon, comparing its pinnacles to the
Giralda Tower of Seville, eighty long years before the Pilgrims landed. Two hundred years elapsed, and then a Spanish priest journeying from the Great Salt Lake reached the
cañon in the very year that witnessed the declaration of

BLACK ROCKS AND YELLOW RAPIDS

American Independence.   Nearly another hundred years
rolled by before our government attempted to probe into the
mystery of the cañon country.   In 1858 Lieutenant Ives
ascended the river from the Gulf of California in a flat-
bottomed steamer, but he did not pass the gateway that
guards the lower end of the Grand Cañon proper.   Twelve
years later, Powell, starting from the north, achieved his
memorable dash, and put to flight uncertainties and mysteries.   Ten years later, Captain Dutton, a geologist who
should have been a man of letters, explored the great plateau
and the side gorges, and described his visions of the cañon in
the language of a poet, delightfully refreshing in a Government Report.   To-day the ablest men of science are solving

THE ARCHEAN CHANNEL

one by one the mighty geologic problems here presented.
And meantime we Americans who pride ourselves upon our
knowledge of the Congo and the upper Nile, who read with
interest descriptions of Siberian deserts and New Zealand
fiords, are asking with languid curiosity: "Where is this
Cañon of the Colorado? What is it like?"

And yet we who have visited it must perforce ask the
same question: What is it like? That is the great question
to which no man can give the answer. It is like no other
thing in heaven or earth; and yet within it are the likenesses
of many notable and famous things. Familiar mountains,
cliffs, and valleys are outlined here by hundreds. An army of
El Capitans, each one as stately as the rock of the Yosemite,

BLACK PALISADES AND PINKISH PINNACLES

Photograph by Sumner W. Matteson

AN ARIZONA CHARON

stand sentry-like on either side.   A thousand miles of palisades, surpassing those that look upon the lordly Hudson,
here serve to form a modest frieze along the rim.   All the
chasms of the world are here in counterfeit, but they appear
like the merest corrugations, grooves, and crinkles.   Niagara
could roar almost unheard in depths that are unseen.   The

AT THE FOOT OF THE GRAND VIEW TRAIL

rivers of our continent could find an ample channel here, yet
leave above their united waters enough to make the cañon
still the wonder of the earth.   Within this gulf the ruins of
all man's masonry since Babel could be hurled, and yet these
Cañon Pyramids whence forty centuries of centuries look
down would rise above the wreck of all the cities of all time!

But after all that can be said is said, one simple fact
stands forth, significant because of its simplicity.   This realm
of wonder and of beauty, vast and intricate though it be, is
the result of simple causes.   It is the natural slow creation
of the flowing waters which drop by drop have traversed it,
reduced its rocks to sand, and borne the sand grain by grain
to the distant all-embracing ocean, where even now the con-
tinents of some far future age are building.

OUT FROM THE CAÑON DEPTHS

APPROACH TO WALPI FROM THE EAST

MOKI LAND

Moki Land

M OKI LAND in Arizona is the home of the strangest of our fellow-countrymen. Moki Land is unique; it is a changeless corner in our land of perpetual change. The Mokis are a pueblo people, differing from other tribes of the southwest in language, customs, and religion. They dwell in seven villages, each set like an acropolis upon a barren rock, high above the barren, boundless sands of the Arizona desert.

How long they have lived there in the sunshine, no man knows. The Spaniards found them there in 1541, living and

praying and performing their religious ceremonies, just as
they had lived and prayed and worshiped for uncounted
centuries.   The conquistadors, seeking only gold and treasure, passed them by, leaving them secure in their unconscious
poverty and in their utter isolation.   To-day we find them
as they were — their pagan civilization still intact.   To-
morrow we may look for it in vain, for the white man presses
closer every year.   If we would see these people still dominated by their immemorial traditions, we must not delay.
Moki Land offers us a fascinating picture of primitive America — a picture that will soon fade in the growing light of our
civilization.   Let us draw aside the protecting curtain of distance and look upon this unique picture before it is too late.

The desert trail that leads to Moki Land touches civilization at a point called Cañon Diablo, about half-way across
the territory of Arizona, on the main line of the Santa Fé.
This station is not far from Flagstaff, the starting-point for
the Grand Cañon of the Colorado.   But at Cañon Diablo
station we see no town, nor a cañon, nor even a devil
to enliven the melancholy desert wastes.   The town has not
been built, the cañon although not far away is invisible,
and the devil prefers to stay in his old home where it is

CAÑON DIABLO STATION
ARIZONA

CAÑON DIABLO

Photograph by H. C. Vroman, Pasadena

probably cooler and more cheerful. This desert is made especially melancholy by the scattering evidences of civilization, —freight-cars, signal-posts, telegraph-poles, and signboards. It is not a sandy desert. It is of rock so firm that poles cannot be planted but must be held erect by pyramids of broken rock piled up around their bases. The only house in town besides the station is the store of Volz, the Indian trader,

AT VOLZ'S STORE
by H. C. Vroman, Pasadena

where we disconsolately discuss the assured discomforts of the trip while awaiting the departure of our caravan. Volz, the trader, has volunteered to be our guide, and has contracted to provide vehicles and horses to transport us to the Moki Reservation about seventy miles away; to feed us on the

by H. C. Vroman, Pasadena   EN ROUTE TO MOKI LAND

best canned goods that ever come to Arizona; to see that we do not lack water more than twelve hours at a stretch; to show us the Snake Dance, give a Navajo Tournament in our honor, and bring us safely back to the railway, all within the incredibly short space of eleven days.

The prospect is alluring; the caravan is ready; let us set out across the almost trackless desert. Our guide has promised much, but the one thing that he failed to mention we find the most inspiring thing of all; the sense of freedom, the exhilaration of this boundless region. It has been said that it is impossible to despair on horseback. This is more than ever true in Arizona, where the air, the light, the clear, sharp distances, and the level, limitless desert form an environment that uplifts the senses and makes for perfect happiness. Let those who choose to do so follow in the lazy wagons, carryalls, and buggies; as for us, we are content only so long as the smooth uncounted miles are flying beneath our horses' willing feet.

The desert is a boundless bridle path, level and to all appearances secure; yet there are pitfalls ranging in size from the burrows of prairie-dogs to the long cracks made by earthquakes.

The first incident of the desert journey is the

Photograph by H. C. Vroman, Pasadena

AN EARTHQUAKE CRACK

fording of the Little Colorado, a shallow, muddy stream as
commonplace as a mere ditch; yet this same river only fifty
miles farther on has cut for itself a cañon of tremendous depth.
When it meets the greater Colorado at the eastern end of

CROSSING THE LITTLE COLORADO

the Grand Cañon, the walls that rise from the bed of the
lesser river meet the walls of the Grand Cañon, as equals in
height and sheerness. The lesser and the greater Colorado
meet in one of the most impressive amphitheaters in the
world, but so remote and difficult
of access is the place, that only
a daring few have looked
upon the scene toward
which these swift and
silent waters are now
gliding.

At noon we halt for
luncheon; but luncheon
is too elegant a term,
even lunch smacks too
much of civilization; the
proper word in Arizona for

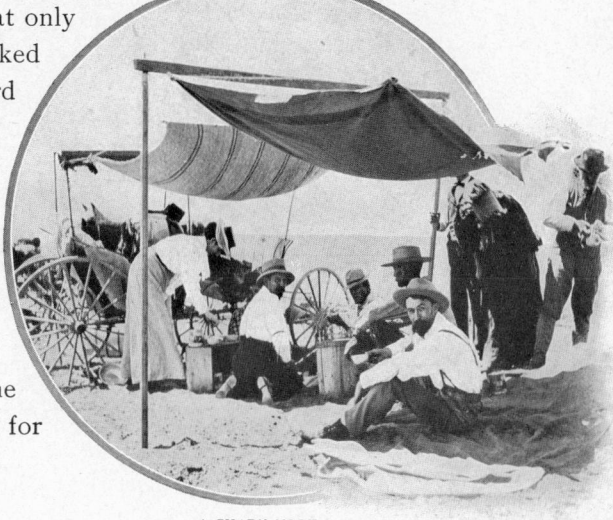

A SHADY NOOK

lunch is "grub." Almost everything one eats comes in a tin
can or tin box; beans, milk, and meat, sardines, preserves,
and jams,—all are imported in hermetically sealed tins. Thus
canned goods form a most important item in the commerce of
the territory, where they are known by the comprehensive
name "air-tights." We breakfast, dine, and sup on air-
tights, and before every meal all hands are set to work with
old knives and scissors, for the rare can-opener is usually missing; and by the time that the air-tights have ceased to de-
serve the title, the workers have in the effort of opening them
already developed appetites ravenous to such a degree that
no time is wasted in vain longings for fresh fare. A heap of
empty tins marks every halting-place of every caravan; while
near the site of every camp are left mountains of gaping cans.
As the Professor from Berlin remarked one day after lunch,
in his staid, scientific tone, "It is my conviction that in a
future age the geologists will be confronted by a novel prob-
lem; for Arizona will be found covered with a stratum of
tin as extensive as the borders of the territory."

We spend the night at a second store belonging to our
trader-guide about thirty miles from the railway. Mr. Volz

Photograph by H. C. Vroman, Pasadena

DISCUSSING "ARIZONA AIR-TIGHTS"

controls three of these establishments, one at the Cañon
Diablo station ; another at a place called by courtesy "The
Lakes," because when it rains, water stands in the broad
hollows that surround this emi-
nence ; and a third store within

THE STORE AT THE LAKES

a few miles of Oraibi, the
largest of the Moki villages,
which is to be our headquarters when we reach the reservation.   We are now in the land
roamed over by the Navajos,
with whom the trader
does a thriving busi-
ness ; for his long
shed is both a sta-
ble and a shop
stocked with the
things in which
the red man de-
lights — tobacco,
matches, pots,
pans, hardware,
and army blankets.
We never weary of

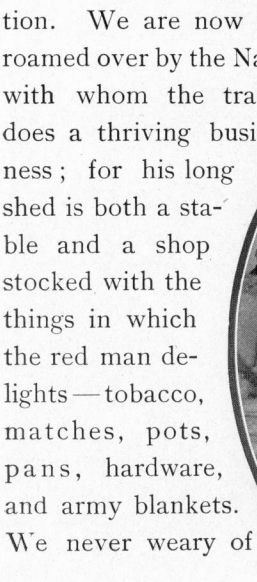

NAVAJO CUSTOMERS

AN EARLY START

watching the transactions. A big brave enters and calls for one pound of soda-crackers. These are weighed out, he wraps them in his blanket, then takes off his belt, and from it pays out—not coins, but—seven cartridges, .44 caliber; and these the clerk sweeps into the cash-drawer without a sign of surprise. Then the same Indian orders another pound of crackers, and pays for them in the same manner as before. He wanted two pounds all the time. But he knows that seven cartridges will buy one pound, and he does not care to venture into deep commercial complications. After business hours the store becomes our dormitory; four men sleep on the counter, two under it, the rest on the floor. We each have new Navajo blankets to use for our bedding;

A DESERT DERELICT

the ladies of our party sleep in a storeroom with a hundred brilliant blankets piled under and around them.

At sunrise the caravan is once more under way, the wagons crawling northward at a tiresome pace, the horsemen galloping ahead, glorying in the splendor of the morning—a morning wider than the world and higher than the sky. We cannot understand how age and misery can afflict humanity

Photograph by H. C. Vroman, Pasadena

BUTTES AND MESAS IN THE ARIZONA DESERT

in an atmosphere like this; we almost feel as if the poor, old Navajo grandmother who comes begging to the store were only feigning decrepitude and poverty. We look for her to toss away her brown rags and gray wig, and to stand forth

Photograph by Sumner W. Matteson BURRO SPRING

in the sunshine radiant in youth and beauty, like the fairy queens seen in pantomimes. We are so light-hearted, filled with the joy of living, that we cannot forgive this old hag for reminding us that in this world there are many blind souls who see no beauty in the earth and sky, who are incapable of happiness. Yet we give her money, for we feel that we owe somebody something because we are *not* miserable; for is there not much truth in that dictum of the cynic who defined "charity" as the "unconscious expression of subconscious fear"? You may smile at this definition if you will, but there is some-

ORAIBI MESA FROM VOLZ'S CAMP

thing fearfully incisive about it—"the unconscious expression of subconscious fear." But away with the old witch who has haunted us! It is as easy to lose a gloomy thought

in Arizona as it is to breathe life-giving air ; and while our
horses gallop on across these endless stretches of sage and
sand, the eye gallops around the huge ring of the horizon,
which now and then is broken by a butte or a mesa, a wall of
sandstone red as brick, regular as a factory façade, wide as a
township, high as the Alhambra of a race of giants.   Now
and then we skirt ephemeral lakes, born of a sudden deluge.
On our return journey we came at nightfall to the shores of a
lake five miles wide, which lay directly across the trail that
we had traversed in dusty dryness only eight days before.
We made a détour of fifteen miles to get around that lake,
and had we not sent back at night to warn a following party,

Photograph by H. C. Vroman, Pasadena

OUR MIDDAY " MESA "

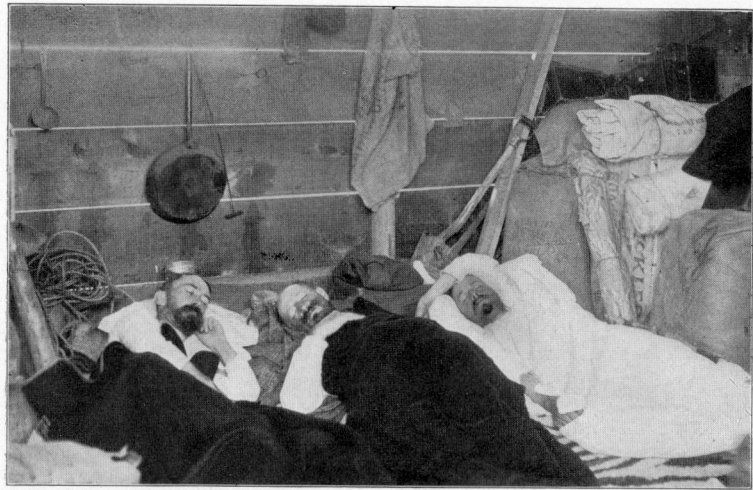

Photograph by H. C. Vroman, Pasadena

SOLID COMFORT

they in attempting to keep to the old trail would have floun-
dered all night in the shallow sea which had dropped from the
clouds in a single day.

Late in the afternoon of our second day in the desert, we
came to Volz's third establishment, the business center of the
Moki Reservation.   First we shake off the dust of our long

Photograph by H. C. Vroman, Pasadena

"WE OURSELVES" AT VOLZ'S STORE

two days' ride, then at a table on an improvised veranda we attack a few dozen tins of air-tights and drink a pail or two of coffee. The amount of coffee that one can consume in Arizona is incredible; it is poured out in bowls, served piping hot, black and without milk. We average two bowls at every meal and sleep like tops. Some of us sleep in tents, others in one of the shanties. We lie in blankets on the

Photograph by Sumner W. Matteson

THE SHOPPING CENTER

bare ground, cases of canned provisions and bales of goods piled high all around us. There are ants in the sand, and we know that rattlesnakes abound, but we are reassured by the knowledge that for four days the Mokis from Oraibi have been scouring the desert collecting rattlers for the Snake Dance ceremony which we have come to witness.

The ladies of our party have more luxurious accommodations. They use as berths the counters and shelves in the adjoining store; but this arrangement has its disadvantages,

16

for they are early routed out because the Indians go shopping
shortly after sunrise, and gather in impatient groups on find-
ing that the shutters of this popular emporium have not been
taken down at the usual hour for beginning the business of
the day.   This counter is the shopping center of all Moki
Land.   The idea seems preposterous, yet Trader Volz
handles every month ten thousand dollars' worth of goods.

One of the first arrivals at our camp is a young Moki,
who wears a gorgeous shirt of multi-colored calico, a shock
of jet-black hair, and a splendid set of teeth framed by a
smile of wide dimensions.   He is an old friend of the trader,
and is frequently employed as a guide to lead the way along
the indistinct old trails that lead across the corn-fields to the
distant mesas and then wind up the steep, rough slopes to
villages set upon the rocky summits.   Corn is the staple prod-
uct of the Moki farmer.   The corn-fields of the Mokis are to
them the most important thing on earth, the object of their
thoughts and prayers.   They tell us that this year the crop
is sure to be a record-breaker, and they point with great
pride to their wide and prosperous fields.   The aspect of a
thriving Moki corn-field
would hardly please a

THE ONLY "SHIRT-WAIST MAN"
IN MOKI LAND

OUR GUIDE

Kansas farmer, but to the Moki it is full of promise. He sees in it the assurance that his village garners will be well filled, that plenty will reign during the winter on the mesa-tops, and he thanks the spirits of the clouds and of the springs for sending a sufficient supply of water to make possible so splendid a result. And his faith in the all-powerful beings that rule the clouds and control the rivers and the springs is deepened, and he is more than ever convinced of the efficacy of the Moki invocations, all of which are intended to propitiate the gods and

A THRIVING CORN-FIELD

A MOKI FARMER

spirits and thus insure abundant water from both earth and sky. The Mokis, when they came to this region at some undated day in the dim past, brought with them corn and beans, squashes, melons, and cotton. We see the squash- and melon-vines crawling about the corn-fields like long green snakes with yellow eyes. Then later, within historic times, wheat, apricots, and peaches were added to their meager list. There are so-called peach-orchards which produce enough small peaches to supply the tribe with its favorite luxury, and leave a little over to be sold to Navajos, or traded for goods at Volz's store. But the farmer's life is one of great

CORN, MELONS, AND SQUASHES

Photograph by Sumner W. Matteson A "PEACH ORCHARD"

uncertainties. The rains, in spite of priestly incantations, sometimes come before they are wanted, or after the need of them has passed, or they come in storm and fury, flood the "washes" and wipe out of existence a corn-field or an orchard, leaving in its place a muddy void.

Even more to be feared are the wind-storms which literally blow away the farms, carrying the surface soil across the desert and depositing it where no culti-vation had been possible hither-to. Thus, farm-ing becomes liter-ally a pursuit — the farmer pur-suing his shifting

COTTONWOODS

farm from place to place. Imagine the complications that
ensue when one farm is deposited immediately on top of
another by the mischievous winds!

Leaving the fields behind us we gallop on for miles across
the desert, a barren, yellow, world-wide avenue from which
the distant mesas rise like heaps of giant paving-stones.
Here and there a leafy cottonwood affords a grateful shelter
from the fierce rays of an August sun. A few drought-defy-
ing plants appear, peeping timidly from the sands, but we
know that dormant seeds are everywhere, needing but the
moist kiss of the infrequent storm to wake them into life.

When the storm-king has swept in furious dark majesty
across the places that were waste, green things, lie thick in
his wake as if a rain of emeralds had fallen. Dry desert beds
are sometimes quickly filled with seas of sunflowers.

But to-day the only sign of life encountered is in the form
of a pair of youthful aborigines, sitting upon the hurricane-

TWO GENTLEMEN OF WALPI

decks of two "ships of the Arizona desert,"—a pair of
desert donkeys.   One of
the donkeys wears a
most dejected mien,
because, as we ob-
serve, he bears the
mark of s h a m e.
His fine long ear
is clipped in token
that his reputation
is not good.   For
every ass who surrep-
titiously eats any of the
precious corn that grows
in the scant Moki fields must
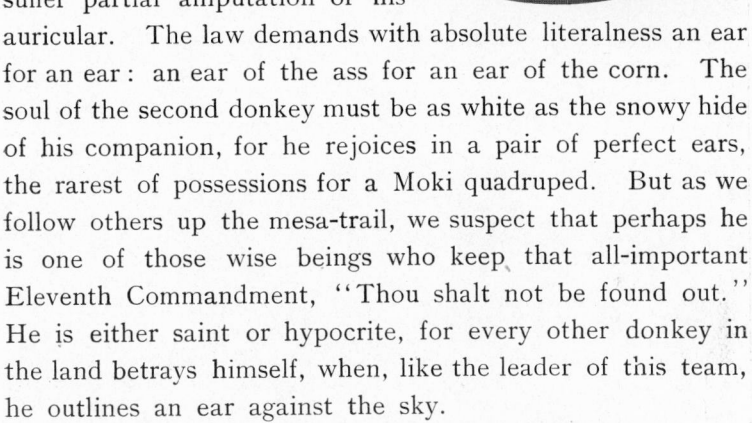
BURROS
suffer partial amputation of his
auricular.   The law demands with absolute literalness an ear
for an ear : an ear of the ass for an ear of the corn.   The
soul of the second donkey must be as white as the snowy hide
of his companion, for he rejoices in a pair of perfect ears,
the rarest of possessions for a Moki quadruped.   But as we
follow others up the mesa-trail, we suspect that perhaps he
is one of those wise beings who keep that all-important
Eleventh Commandment, "Thou shalt not be found out."
He is either saint or hypocrite, for every other donkey in
the land betrays himself, when, like the leader of this team,
he outlines an ear against the sky.

Meantime our guide rides on ahead.   Presently he draws
rein, and pointing to the summit of the mesa exclaims,
"There, Walpi."   Yes, but where is the town of Walpi?
We know it stands upon this sandstone mesa—but we are
not yet able to distinguish it.   The steep slope terminates in
what appears to be a mass of titanic blocks of stone

resembling a natural citadel. Perhaps the town lies on the other side. But no, the guide insists that we are very near ; and when a moment later our horses stumble round another angle of the trail, the cyclopean citadel resolves itself into a Moki village. What seemed gigantic cubes of stone are small pueblo dwellings. Walpi, which from below was indistinguishable, reveals itself as a place of human habitation only to those who scale the cliffs. A caravan of wanderers lost in the desert, dying of thirst, might skirt the bases of these Moki mesas and gaze squarely up at these high-perched dwellings without divining that just overhead men who would give aid and succor lived in populous towns where plenty of food and water and many comforts could be found.

A PUEBLO CITADEL

THE EAST MESA

Photograph by H. C. Vroman, Pasadena

And this town of Walpi on the east mesa, like the six other Moki towns, is the abode of full-fledged citizens of the United States, men who possess the right to vote, but who have never deigned to exercise their franchise ; nor in truth have they been urged to do so.   They were made citizens by the treaty with Mexico, when this territory became a part of the United States after the war of 1845.

The Mokis are good citizens.   It has been said, I know, that the only good Indian is a dead Indian.   In fact, the name "Moki," which we now erroneously apply to this little nation, means literally "dead people," and was originally a term of derision given by the warlike Apaches and Navajos to these peaceful farmers and home-builders.   Ask one of the boys whom we find playing in the Plaza of Walpi what he is, and he will say that he belongs to the "Hopi,"

or "good peo-
ple," for Hopi is
the original name
by which these
P u e b l o-builders
call themselves,
although the term
"Moki," once an
insult, has almost
lost its derisive
meaning and is
not seriously re-
sented.

This p l a z a,
now deserted ex-
cept for a few idle
boys, b e c o m e s
every second year
the theater of the

ON THE WALPI TRAIL

famous Snake Dance ceremony. The sacred Dance Rock rises on the left; the entrance to one of the sacred chambers, where the secret ceremonies are performed, is at our feet. But to-day the town appears deserted. Another

Photograph by Sumber W. Matteson
WALPI — AN ARIZONA ACROPOLIS

village will this year celebrate the Snake Dance. Walpi is as quiet as Oberammergau during the off-years between the presentations of the Passion Play. We shall see it under a different aspect when we return to witness the Snake Dance of 1899, to which we are invited by the great man of the village, Kopele, the chief priest of the Snake Fraternity, the leader of the dance in preceding presentations.

Kopele did not live to greet us when we returned to his pueblo one year later. In him the Hopi lost one whom they called a "*pas lolomá taka*," an "excellent man," whose heart was good and whose speech was straight. Among the whites he was liked and respected as a gentle, courageous, and, as he looked at things, a deeply religious man.

After exploring his village, driving timid children into houses and up to roof-terraces, we set out for the middle mesa. On the descending trail we meet what at first sight appears to be an animated cottonwood. Our horses shy as the big leafy mass comes staggering up the slope, but as it passes we see that the tree-trunk is made of two brown Hopi legs, and from the moving bower comes this Hopi

Photograph by Sumner W. Matteson
WALPI FROM BELOW
SHOWING A MELON-VINE ANCHORED WITH A STONE AND A PEACH-TREE STANDING ON TIP-TOE

greeting: "*Um ha kamii.*" The man is bringing leafy boughs for use in one of the approaching ceremonies.

Farther on we meet a successful rabbit-hunter, who has bagged his game after the Hopi fashion, killing it by a clever

THE WALPI "DANCE ROCK"

throw of a sort of boomerang, in the use of which these
people, owing to constant practice, are most skilful.

A dash across the desert brings us to the base of the middle mesa, around which we toil over rough ground, seeking
a trail by which we may ascend. Secure, indeed, were the
sites selected by the "good people" for their villages when
they fled from the roving Apaches, the Bedouins of the
desert, and set their houses on the rocky slopes. Then, in
the sixteenth century, strange white men clad in armor came
from the distant south. They were the Spanish conquistadors, sent by Coronado to seek the Seven Cities of Cibola,
thought to be rich in treasure. They found these pueblo

towns upon the mesas. They tried to enter; Moki priests
protested and with sacred meal drew a line across the path.
The Spaniards then bombarded with blunderbuss and bowgun,
killing several Mokis. Next day the frightened mesa folk
brought down gifts, welcomed the masterful strangers, and
consented to build a church. The conquerors passed on,
leaving a few priests to rule the Hopi villages. The people
did not object to Christianity until the priests declared that
all the gods of the Hopi were evil gods. This blasphemy
roused the peaceful people, and they threw the "long

Photograph by H. C. Vroman, Pasadena

HOPI ARCHITECTURE

gowns," as they called the friars, over the edge of the mesa,
destroyed the church, moved their villages to securer heights
upon the mesa tops, and when another Spanish expedition
came, they attempted to defy the power of the white man.

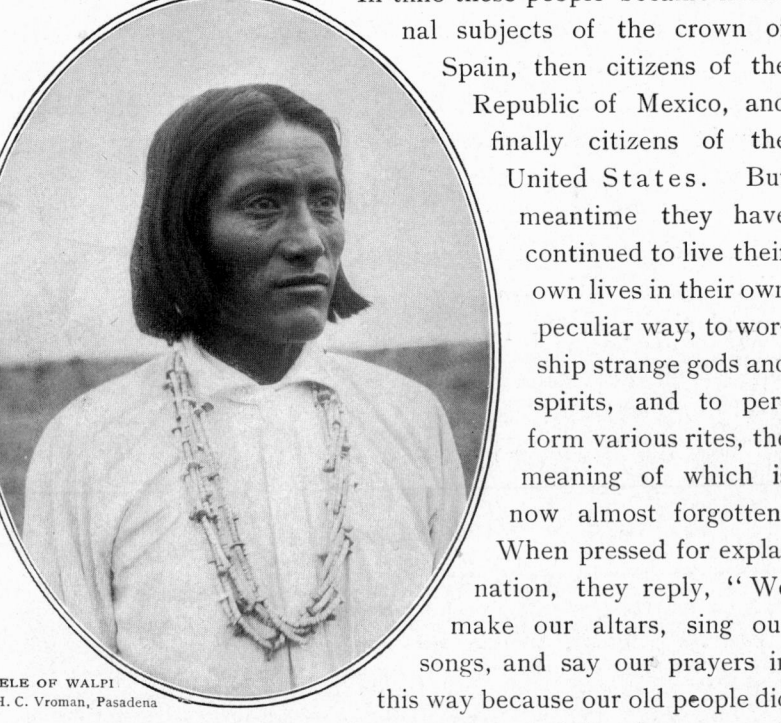

KOPELE OF WALPI
Photograph by H. C. Vroman, Pasadena

In time these people became nomi-
nal subjects of the crown of
Spain, then citizens of the
Republic of Mexico, and
finally citizens of the
United States. But
meantime they have
continued to live their
own lives in their own
peculiar way, to wor-
ship strange gods and
spirits, and to per-
form various rites, the
meaning of which is
now almost forgotten.
When pressed for expla-
nation, they reply, " We
make our altars, sing our
songs, and say our prayers in
this way because our old people did
so ; and surely they knew how to make rain fall and corn grow."

Doubtless the Moki girls looked down upon the Spaniards
with the same air of timid daring they exhibit to-day as we
approach the village. If we are to credit the Spanish chron-
iclers, the Moki maiden then wore her hair in the same
fantastic form, and clad herself in the quaint, picturesque
garments of which those of to-day are perfect counterparts.

Only the decrepit old men are found at home by day ;
the active male population is in the distant fields guarding
the corn, the melons, and the beans, leaving the village in
possession of the aged, the women, and the children. At
our first approach the children fled like a lot of prairie-dogs,
popping into the underground rooms, or *kivas*, dashing
through low doorways into cube-like dwellings, or running up

"ERANGED" RABBITS
aph by Sumner W. Matteson

the ladders to the housetops. There
they are free to wander all over town,
leaving to us the empty streets and
deserted plazas. A pueblo village is practically one structure.
The streets and alleyways are
roofed with rooms; the entrance to one house is often
found upon the roof of the
dwelling of a neighbor. There
are ladders and stone stairways
everywhere, and these are used
more generally than the streets
and squares below. This village
is called Mishongnovi. In the distance looms a higher village which is
called Shipaulovi, "the Place of the Peaches." A third
village on this mesa bears the name of Shungopavi.

The people of each village are divided into many clans,
and each clan is regarded as a family. Its members may not

Photograph by Sumner W. Matteson
ROCK PICTURE OF A RABBIT HUNT

17

intermarry ; they must wed the sons and daughters of some other clan. There are seven villages in all. The natives number about twenty-five hundred, of whom eight hundred live in Oraibi, which is the largest of the villages. Evidently the population is

NATURE'S ARCHITECTURE

increasing, for as soon as we produce big bags of colored candies and begin a distribution, young Hopi hopefuls begin to spring up like desert weeds under the influence of a sudden deluge. A few minutes of this bombardment of bonbons, and all

A TRYING TRAIL

THE SNAKE DANCE AT WALPI

Photograph by H. C. Vroman, Pasadena

timidity is banished. We are accepted as "good people," and the entire village is ours to explore, to ransack, and to photograph. First the young girls who ran away like startled deer at sight of the strange visitors, gather in hesitating groups and do their best to "look pleasant."

APPROACH TO THE MIDDLE MESA

We notice that the dress of the girls and old women is identical: a heavy blanket-like robe, the black body separated from the dark blue border by stripes of brilliant green. Around the waist is worn a woven sash. All these things are of domestic manufacture; in fact, the men do all the dress-making,—the husband always weaving the wedding garment for the bride,—but weaving it so well that it will last the wife

a lifetime, and then possibly serve a daughter until marriage.
The shawls of brilliant calico, however, are purchased from
the trader.   The most striking feature in the make-up of the

Photograph by H. C. Vroman, Pasadena

HOPI FLATS

Hopi girl is her coiffure, unique among the world's hair-
dressing schemes.   Fantastic as it appears when built up
with the black hair of the brown brunettes, its queerness is
intensified when it is formed of the snowy tresses of the pale
Albino maidens.   There is something uncanny about the
three or four pale-faced, white-haired, and pink-eyed creat-
ures who haunt these towns like Hopi ghosts, doubly con-
spicuous in this black-haired, dark-eyed population.   The
younger girls and also many of the men wear their hair cut

in the fashion of the medieval Florentines,—a heavy bang on the brow, and a curtain of black tresses covering the ears and neck. The jewelry worn by the Hopi folk is marvelous; silver beads and pendants purchased from the Navajos, strings of shells with bits of common turquoise interspersed, earrings of silver inlaid with turquoise, and silver rings and bracelets chiseled with strange Navajo designs. But all the brilliant trappings of the Hopi débutante cannot distract our attention from her crowning glory. We never cease to

HOPI HOPEFULS

marvel at the abundance and the jet-black splendor of her hair. We ask if, like the Japanese, these girls are forced when sleeping to rest the neck on wooden pillows to prevent a disarrangement of the

NAVAJO
CHILDREN
PLAYING
HORSE

elaborate coiffure ; but we are told that it is combed out every night and freshly built up every morning, with the assistance of a mother or a friend. We wonder if this fashion will ever reach the cities of the States. Here is a hint for women who are seeking something new.

Photographs by Sumner W. Matteson
KIDS

Photograph by H. C. Vroman, Pasadena
CANDY HAS COME

Unfortunately I cannot tell you how the trick is done, but possibly the two American ladies at one of the missions on the reservation can enlighten you. I know they are in possession of the secret, for we found them one day togged out in full Hopi ceremonial costume, with their hair done up in proper Hopi style. An educated Hopi named Luke is with them who, nevertheless, being a member of the Snake Fraternity, will later appear in the barbaric attire of a Hopi priest, and chant the meaningless songs of the ancients, and carry rattlesnakes

THE PASSING STRANGER

between his teeth. Tradition rules this people. The Hopi will admit that the things we try to teach him are "good medicine," but he remains a Snake Man still, and follows faithfully the teaching of his tribe. After marriage the women uncoil those flaring ears of hair and let two tresses dangle; the young girls wear the hair done up, older women let it hang, just the reverse to our familiar custom.

Photograph by H. C. Vroman, Pasadena
HOW THE HOPI MAIDEN'S HAIR IS DRESSED

The babies of Moki Land lead a happy life. Water is so precious here that none is wasted in those unnecessary and annoying scrubbings. The tub has no terrors for the urchins of these towns. They bathe only in the clear dry air, wash their faces in sunshine, comb their hair with the sharp wind from the desert, and are as healthy as the children of the poor in any land. They are wonderfully self-reliant. The town is an intricate apartment-house with steep stairways and tall crude ladders as the only means of communication between floor and floor. But babies that can barely creep on level ground develop at a very early age a daring familiarity with the ups and downs of life. Bronze babies are found everywhere. Some one has called them "Fried Cupids," and as in other lands these cupids rule the house.

Photograph by H. C. Vroman, Pasadena
THE HAIR-DRESSING CONTINUED

The Hopi home is not at all unhomelike.   The
houses are well built of stone,
with neatly plastered walls,
thick sun-defying roofs of
mud, and many doors
and windows which ad-
mit fresh air and sun-
shine. Cooking is done
in fireplaces not unlike
our own, and the smoke
is carried off through
chimneys most ingen-
iously contrived. To
make a Moki chim-
ney, take a lot of di-

Photograph by H. C. Vroman, Pasadena
THE HAIR-DRESSING CONTINUED

lapidated water-jars, knock out the bottoms, plaster up the
cracks, and pile them jar on jar until the chimney is of sufficient height, and then build the house around the chimney.
The English idea of the "chimney-pot" is not a new one
to the Indian.   Interiors are usually very clean and tidy, the
walls and floors are frequently plastered with clay ; a ledge
runs around each room, affording sitting space for many
guests ; long poles are hung with brilliant blankets made by
the neighboring Navajos, and
high shelves are loaded with
quaint pottery.   In a corner
are the inclined stones
where women sit to grind
the corn, and overhead is
the well-constructed roof
of beams and thatch, sup-
porting a layer of
sun-baked mud.   A
peep into another

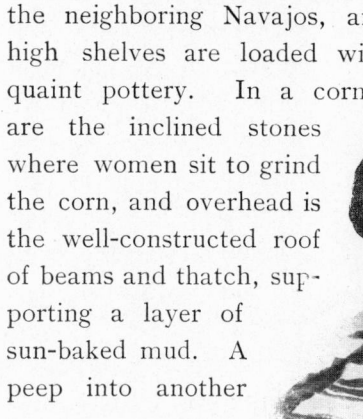

Photograph by H. C. Vroman, Pasadena
THE HAIR-DRESSING COMPLETED

MOKI LAND COIFFURES

room reveals a brave array of melons and of decorated bowls heaped high with white corn-meal. Saddles, bridles, and a sombrero, tell that the master owns a pony, while a decaying grip-sack tells of a journey made once upon a time. Above our heads is a feather dangling from a string. This is the soul of the house; no dwelling is without it.

The Moki house is always the property of the wife; she has the right to order her

Photograph by Sumner W. Matteson
WON'T WEAR EVEN BEADS

lord and master out of doors if he does not
behave himself, but this she rarely does.

The Hopi are indeed "good people";
they do not gamble, and, strange to say,
they do not drink. They scarcely know
the taste of fire-water, and the conscien-
tious trader is determined that they shall
not know the red man's curse. The
men are usually industrious, spending
much time in the fields, planting,
building dikes, digging ditches.
Weaving is about their only
indoor occupation. All house-

"AND THE MOTHER AND THE CHILD WERE THERE"

hold duties are per-
formed by the women,
and the Moki woman's
hardest task is to carry
water from the spring
some five hundred feet
below, near the rocky
foundation of the mesa.
These springs yield the
water sparingly drop by
drop, and in the dryer
season the part of Re-
becca at the well is one
to try the patience even
of the unhurried Moki

WASHED IN SUNSHINE ONLY

A HOPI INTERIOR

A HOPI HOME

TOKENS OF PROSPERITY

matron. Her lightest task is chewing the yeast for fermenting
the batter to make the Moki's favorite dish — corn-pudding.

AT THE DAILY GRIND

We declined all invitations to dine out, though we did taste the Moki bread, called "*piki*," which looks like lavender tissue-paper; it is made from purple corn, ground and mixed with water, and cooked into crisp sheets on hot, flat stones. We find in nearly every house a number of the curious dolls called "*katcinas*." These figures represent certain mythic

CORN-MEAL AND MELONS

deities of the Hopi pantheon. They are given to the children as an object-lesson in their intricate religion, to teach the little ones to know their gods by sight. At certain seasons festivals in honor of these gods are held, and full-grown men dressed to resemble these strange beings appear upon the streets wearing fantastic masks.

Photograph by Sumner W. Matteson
HOPI HYDRAULICS

Moki Land also boasts of many other ceremonies that are unique and beautiful and thrilling, but little is said of these because of the sensational import of the Snake Dance.

We learned of many interesting, unfamiliar things from a missionary at Oraibi, a German gentleman representing the Russian Mennonite Society. During the five years of his stay his mission-house was made a veritable museum of curious Hopi paraphernalia. Each year he added to it some priceless bowl, or talisman, or mask, some sacred wand, or a quaint katcina doll, until this wonderful collection could not be left any longer in

Photograph by Sumner W. Matteson
WATER JARS AWAITING A SUPPLY OF WATER SUFFICIENT TO FILL THEM

18

Photograph by Sumner W. Matteson

BAKING PIKI BREAD

the far-away Arizona desert, never seen save by the infrequent tourist.   Thanks to the generosity of a young million-
aire, these invaluable illustrations of the Hopi rites and social
customs have been transferred to the Field Columbian
Museum, in Chicago, where to-day the student may find an
epitome of Hopi life.   In addition to the Mennonite and
several other missions there is a gov-
ernment school at the foot of
every mesa.   School does not
keep in summer, but we
camped in a school-house
during our visit to the
middle mesa, and ate the
two poor teachers out of
house and home.   They
told us that the opening
exercises during school-terms

Photograph by H. C. Vroman, Pasadena
THE DAUGHTER OF THE HOUSE

consisted in a detailed scrubbing of every member of the
infant class with government soap and precious water from
the springs.   The Hopi look upon this wasteful ceremony as
proof that white people are insane.   It is to them far more
ridiculous than their invocations to the gods for rain can ever
seem to us.   We did not have an opportunity to study the
results of government instruction.   The bathing habit does
not become fixed, and I doubt if the a, b, c, or even the

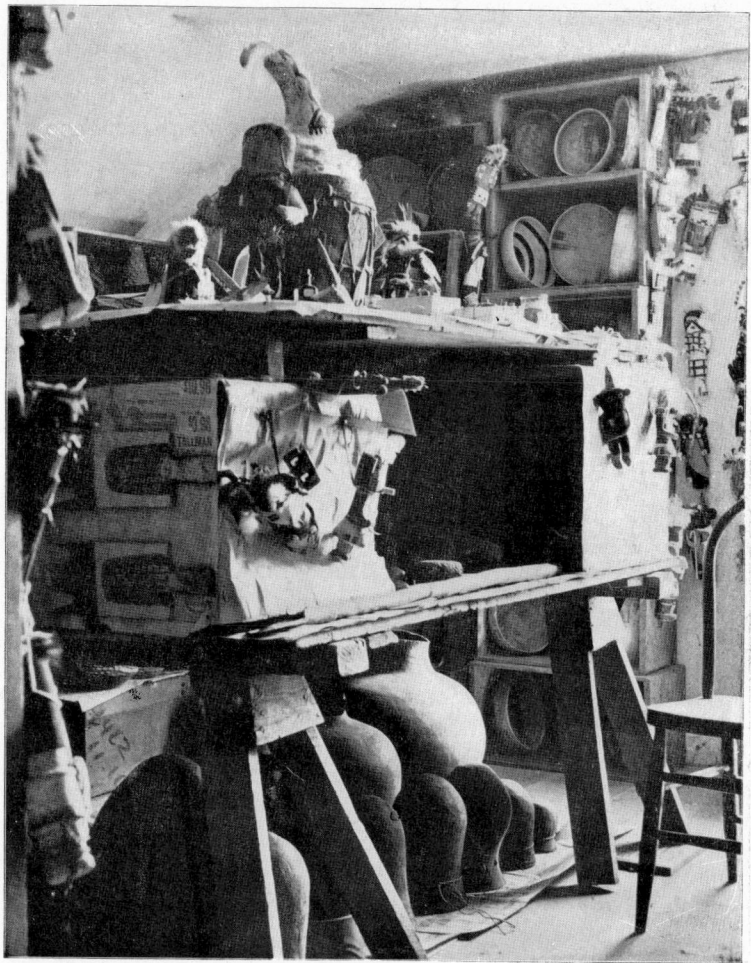

THE REV. MR. VOTH'S COLLECTION AT THE MISSION

multiplication-table takes deeper
root.   How can they, when
the teachers sent to train
the infant Indians are not
obliged to learn the
language of the peo-
ple? What progress
is possible with the
barrier of language
between pupil and
preceptor?

The Snake Dance of
1898 was performed in
August at Oraibi. Though
Oraibi is the largest town of
Moki Land, it is at the same time
the one least in touch with the white man's civilization.
Walpi has long been accustomed to the visits of strangers

MOKI SPOONING
LOVER BUSY KNITTING
HIS INAMORATA HOLDING HIS FOOT
Photograph by Sumner W. Matteson

Photograph by H. C. Vroman, Pasadena

A GOVERNMENT SCHOOL

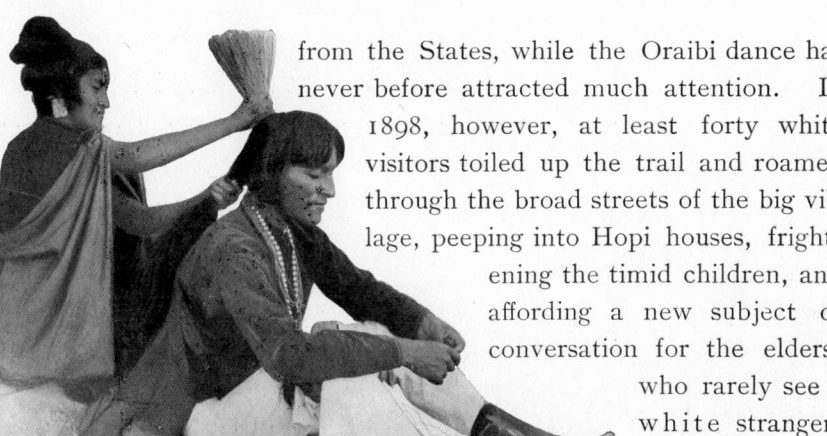

from the States, while the Oraibi dance has never before attracted much attention. In 1898, however, at least forty white visitors toiled up the trail and roamed through the broad streets of the big village, peeping into Hopi houses, frightening the timid children, and affording a new subject of conversation for the elders, who rarely see a white stranger. Subjects of conversation, by the way, are few in Moki Land; but never-failing topics are the lack of water, the condition

Photograph by Sumner W. Matteson
BRUSHING BROTHER'S HAIR

of the springs, and the possibility of a copious downpour in response to the invocations of the priests. The one thought uppermost in Hopi minds is how to bring the rains down from the passing clouds upon the thirsty fields and into their empty reservoirs and cisterns. The whole complicated symbolism of their religion illustrates this never absent aspiration. The ceremonies we are soon to witness, however vague their meaning may appear, are all performed by a believing people to the end that springs may flow abundantly, that copious rains may fall, and that bounteous crops of corn and beans and melons may grow up out of the desert sands.

Photograph by Sumner W. Matteson
QUEN-CHOW-A

For nine days the village has been wrapped in mystery. Meetings of immemorial societies have been held in the chambers underground, called *"kivas,"* the entrances to which are accented by projecting ladder-poles. The Antelope and Snake societies sit in solemn conclave in

RIDING TO ORAIBI

their respective kivas, chanting old songs, the meanings of which were long ago forgotten. Should we venture into those dark refuges and look upon forbidden things, we should, according to the Hopi belief, swell up and burst instantly. But in spite of this awful danger, many of these secret rites, so long and tedious, have been very carefully studied by American ethnologists, some of whom have been made members of the societies, and admitted to

Photograph by Sumner W. Matteson
DRAWING WATER FROM A CISTERN

THE WASHING OF THE SNAKES

Photograph by Sumner W. Matteson

the most solemn and utterly unspeakable séances. But
the minute details recorded by the scientists do not interest the casual visitor, intent on the broad picturesqueness
of the public ceremony. While these invisible doings are
in progress underground, other strange things are happen-
ing in the wide desert round about. Each day for seven
days swift, naked runners are sent out to carry *bahos*, or

ORAIBI

prayer-offerings, to distant shrines. The first messenger
speeds on foot around the mesa, describing a circuit of
twenty-five miles; but each succeeding day the circle
shrinks, until on the last day the runner closely skirts the
town itself, depositing his tokens in the nearby shrines. The
wider circuit is made that the rain-clouds hiding far away
may see and be attracted, and then may be lead nearer and
nearer as the runner shortens his course, until they can hear

Photograph by Sumner W. Matteson

CONSECRATING "BAHOS" IN THE ANTELOPE KIVA

the prayers of the people in the villages. Hopi men and boys are famous for their fleetness. One who was employed

Flash-light photograph by Sumner W. Matteson

SNAKE PRIESTS SLEEPING ON THE KIVA ROOF

SNAKE MEN

by Volz to bring him news of the priestly proclamation fixing the exact date of the dance, ran to the railway at Cañon Diablo and back again to his village, a distance of one hundred and fifty miles, in twenty-five hours; all this in loose ankle-deep

RETURNING FROM THE FIRST DAY'S HUNT

Photograph by Sumner W. Matteson
A SHRINE WITH OFFERINGS OF FEATHERS AND BAHOS

sand. It may be said for comparison that the same journey, including only such stops as were necessary for sleep and food, cost us four days of horseback travel.

But while the circling messengers are propitiating the spirits of the shrines, other men set out to seek other mes-

Photograph by Sumner W. Matteson
SNAKE HUNTERS LEAVING THE KIVA ON THE FIRST DAY'S HUNT, TO THE NORTH

Photograph by Sumner W. Matteson

"ANTELOPE MAID" AND "SNAKE YOUTH" IN ANTELOPE KIVA AT FOUR A. M. ON THE NINTH DAY OF THE SNAKE CEREMONY

Photograph by Sumner W. Matteson

THE SNAKE HUNT TO THE WEST

sengers more pleasing to the greater spirits who control the
hydraulics of the sky. These messengers are snakes ; the

Photograph by Sumner W. Matteson

THE SNAKE HUNT TO THE EAST

rattlesnake is called " chief " because it is most efficacious in bringing rain.   For four days snakes are hunted far and wide, first to the north, then to the west, south, and east. The men are armed with sticks and hoes, and carry little bags in which they gently place their wriggling captives.

Photograph by Sumner W. Matteson

PRIESTS SMOKING AND PRAYING AROUND THE SACRED FIRE THE NIGHT PREVIOUS TO THE PUBLIC HANDLING OF THE SNAKES

The reptile-gatherers are never followed.   It would be injurious to follow, and is an omen of evil-fortune even to meet them in the desert.   During their

RED-ROBED WATCHERS

long forays, the fields are deserted. The lay population
remains in town, at home.

On the eighth day
after the commence-
ment of the ceremo-
nies a sort of public
rehearsal of the
dance is held ; but in
place of snakes the
priests use the melon-
vines and corn-stalks.

SUNRISE
SPECTATORS

ON THE ROCKY " GRAND STAND "

This is called the Antelope Dance, because the Antelope
Fraternity directs it.   Then on the morning of the great
ninth day the village is astir long before the sun has peeped
above the desert rim.   The populace robed in brilliant
blankets stand like aboriginal cardinals on the mesa roofs

19

and peer eagerly toward the corn-fields, whence strange cries come now and then. All eyes are riveted on something in the lower distance, something that is moving, for these intently gazing faces slowly turn from left to right. At last the round sun rises and casts over

WATCHING THE RACERS

ADMONISHING
WINNER HOW T
DEPOSIT HIS PR
A BLESSING TO
FIELD AND CRO

the desert a light that looks like pinkish dust. And then, following the eager glance of this assembled multitude, we presently distinguish a dozen figures in the distance running toward us. The "sunrise race" is on, the young men are contending for the honor of being the first to bring a sacred token from the fields. The token is a gourd filled with water. It is snatched from hand to hand as the runners overtake one another. On they come, fleet

Photographs by Sumner W. Matteson

A PRIEST REWARDS THE WINNER

as antelopes in spite of the retarding sands, then up the broken
surface of the trail as if it were a level track, then through the
admiring crowds gathered above, and finally to the door of
the Antelope Kiva where the victor is rewarded by a priest
who recites before him some mysterious words of praise or

THE "CORN-LADS" CLIMBING TO ORAIBI

compliment, and bestows upon him the gourd which the
victor buries in his own field to ensure its future fertility.

Meantime we have discovered hiding amid the rocks a
numerous company of younger boys fantastically arrayed, or
rather unarrayed. Some, it is true, wear scanty rags, but
most of them wear nothing but a coat of paint applied to
face and arms and body. They carry long green stalks of

THE RUSH OF THE "CORN LADS"

corn and little bells which begin to jingle joyfully when, a
moment later, these lurking corn-lads suddenly pop from the
recesses in the cliff and go clambering skyward, waving their
green banners.   Arriving on the level mesa-top they form
in companies and charge toward the village where, massed

SNAKE PRIESTS ENTERING THEIR KIVA

THE PLAZA OF THE SNAKE DANCE AT WALPI.

upon a mound, the women and girls of Oraibi are eagerly awaiting their approach. As soon as the advancing boys are near enough for the girls to see the whites of their laughing eyes, a counter charge is made ; a phalanx of femininity sweeps down upon the army of corn-bearing lads and there ensues

Photograph by Sumner W. Matteson

CLOUD, CORN, LIGHTNING, AND RAIN SYMBOLS

a scrimmage, which recalls a cane-rush.   The object of the
girls is to wrest the cornstalks from the hands of the troup
of boys and then to take them from one another.

A few hours later the Snake Priests, who have been
chanting weird songs in the kiva of the Antelope Society, file
out from that mysterious council-cave, crossing the plaza, and
disappear through the trap-door of their own kiva, where the

Photograph by Sumner W. Matteson

AFTER THE WASHING

snakes are now in close confinement.   Few white men have
ever been permitted to witness the secret rites performed in
these dark kivas.   To-day the most impressive of them all
is celebrated — the ceremony of the washing of the snakes.
After these priests have entered let us in imagination follow
them into the dark recesses of that forbidden den.

The privileged observer, to whom we are indebted for the
unique pictures of the kiva ceremonies, reports that after the

Photograph by Sumner W. Matteson

SNAKE YOUTHS TOYING WITH RATTLERS

priests, with many impressive ceremonial details and much
weird chanting, had dipped the snakes one by one into a
bowl of charm-liquid, they threw them across the kiva and
brushed them about in the colored sands which had been
used in making a symbolic sand-mosaic upon the altar.
Then the reptiles were put into a large bag in which they are
carried to the public ceremony.   The weird horror of the

Photograph by Sumner W. Matteson
DRYING THE SOUSED SNAKES IN THE SUN

scene, impossible to convey in words, is suggested by the
pictures which successfully reveal several of the dramatic
episodes of this frightful pagan rite.

Above ground in the plaza stands what is called the "*kisi*,"
a tent-like structure of cottonwood boughs faced with corn-
stalks.   It has been set up by the priests on the eighth day.
In this a man will be concealed with the capture of snakes,

and from the kisi he will hand them to the dancers one by one at the required moment. The plaza is still practically empty and remains thus until the sun has almost reached the western edge of Moki Land. Then in the fading light specta-tors soon gather ; photographers, cinematograph-

Photograph by H. C. Vroman, Pasadena
BUILDING THE KISI

ers, and chronomatographers unlimber their

THE PHOTOGRAPHIC BATTERY

heavy batteries, while kodakers and snap-shoot-ers maneuver for a favorable posi-tion. But the sun, already low will set before its time ; for in the west is rising a dense black bank of cloud, as if to foil these impious intruders, and at the same time as-sure the priests of

ENTRY OF THE ORAIBI SNAKE PRIESTS

Photograph by Sumner W. Matteson

the Hopi that the rain-clouds have heard the prayers and are
marshaling their forces to give a thunderous answer to the
final and supreme invocation which the priests are soon to
make. Longer and longer grow the shadows, but before
they merge into the shades of twilight, there comes an expectant murmur from the crowd, and a moment later the
pagan priesthoods are all in their places and are ready to
begin their solemn and dramatic invocations.

Photograph by H. C. Vroman, Pasadena
THE ANTELOPE PRIESTS

First, nine members of the Antelope Society rise one by
one from out of the earth, and march with rapid measured
strides four times around the plaza. Then, standing in a line
with backs turned to the kisi, they await the advent of their
brothers of the Snake Fraternity. The pause gives us an
opportunity to study their elaborate make-up. A picture

tells more in an instant than words could tell in half a day.
Embroidered cotton sashes are the most salient features of
their uniform. Long fox-skins hang behind them from the
waist, necklaces and bracelets are seen on necks and arms,
and in their hands they carry little rattles. Upon bare arms
and legs are zigzag marks of pasty clay, symbols of lightning; tied near the knees are rattles made of tortoise shells

Photograph by H. C. Vroman, Pasadena

THE SNAKE PRIESTS

to imitate the sound of thunder, while lines are drawn like
mustaches from ear to ear, and the ears are hid by flowing
tresses. They wear their hair like this "because the rain-
clouds wear their tresses so." The chief priest stands
nearest to us; at his feet we see a thick feathery wand called
a "*tiponi*," the badge of his sacred office. The second
priest in line is the asperger, who sprinkles the charm-

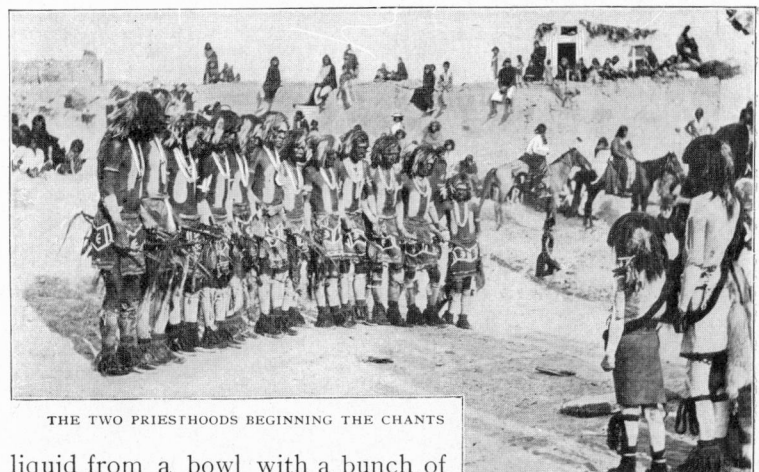

THE TWO PRIESTHOODS BEGINNING THE CHANTS

liquid from a bowl with a bunch of eagle-feathers. He is distinguished by the crown of leaves upon his venerable head. Then come six other priests and one little novice, admitted this year for the first time to participation in the dance. Meantime the Snake Men have appeared, marched round four times, and taken their position.

THE SNAKE CEREMONY AT ORAIBI

The wooden board lying on the ground just in front of the Antelope Men, covers a shallow hole called "*sipapu*," the entrance to the underworld. Every time a priest passes the sipapu he stamps upon it to give assurance to dead

Photograph by Sumner W. Matteson
WITH EARNEST PAGAN PIETY

ancestors that the clan is faithfully performing this immemorial rite appointed by the fathers in the forgotten past. And now comes the first movement of the dance itself,—but the word "dance" conveys a wrong impression. This is a symbolic ceremony, not a dance. The two fraternities begin a low peculiar chant, swaying their bodies, waving their feather wands, pointing them at the ground. The humming chant is almost wordless; it represents the sighing of the winds, the rushing of the storm-clouds, while the accompanying rattles play an obligato as of thunder. There is in it all a mystery and dignity which cannot be described. The movements may at first appear too grotesque, but they are grimly so; the Hopi mystics are never without that dignity peculiar to the children of the desert. The costume of the Snake brothers differs from that of the Antelopes. The kilt is of brown leather with designs of white. Upon the breasts are blotches instead of stripes of clay. Each man carries in one hand a little bag containing sacred corn-meal, in the other a wand of wood with eagle-feather tips. Before attemping to pick up a rattlesnake the priest throws a pinch of meal toward the setting sun, then another upon the coiling snake.

A snake must coil before it can spring and strike; the secret of safety lies in the skill with which the priest induces

Photograph by H. C. Vroman, Pasadena
THE PRELIMINARY CHANT — ORAIBI

the rattler to uncoil. He tickles it deftly with the eagle-feather wand, and the snake, knowing by instinct that the stroke of an eagle's wing always precedes the grip of the eagle's fatal claw, quickly uncoils and squirms away in search of hole or refuge. Once straightened out he may be picked

20

GRIPPING THE REP-
TILES WITH TEETH
AND FINGERS

Photograph by H. C. Vroman, Pasadena

up with impuni-
ty. As the dance
proceeds, you
will see some of
the priests take
snakes of various
kinds from the
kisi, then, hold-
ing the neck be-
tween the teeth
and the body in
the hands, dance
slowly round and
round, followed
by other priests
whose duty is to aid the carrier
in case of need, and to gather up
the wriggling snakes
and prevent their es-
cape, after they have
been dropped upon
the ground. Invari-
ably the gatherer first
throws a pinch of
meal toward the sun
and then one upon
the snake, strokes it
with a feathery wand,
and then with a gest-
ure swift as light he
seizes it and adds it
to the wriggling clus-
ter clutched in his left
hand. Meantime the

BARBARIC
BRAVERY

Photograph by H. C. Vroman, Pasadena

GATHERERS

Photograph by Sumner W. Matteson

ANTELOPE SAND-PAINTING

other priests are chanting and swaying their dark bodies to and fro. One by one, the snakes, about sixty in number, many of them venomous rattlers, are carried round the plaza, dropped on the ground, and gathered in by watchful following priests.

One of the latter, angered because white visitors have approached too near the kisi, vents his spite upon a lady spectator, an artist, who stands near the circling priests, resting a canvas-covered stretcher on the ground as a sort of barrier to ward off the crawling snakes which now and then

ALTAR IN THE ANTELOPE KIVA DURING THE DANCE

glide toward the timorous onlookers. The
gatherer resents her fortified attitude,
and each time that he picks up a
snake, he swings it nearer and nearer
to her face in an attempt to frighten
her into retreat.   But he tries this
once too often, for a final bold
attempt to twine the reptile round
her neck is met by a counter-
attack.   The artist lifts her stout
stretcher, swings it valiantly above
her head as a protection, and brings
it down *smack* on the head of the
astonished Snake Man !

INVOKING THE
LIGHTNING
Photograph by
Sumner W. Matteson

Meantime, women with baskets of corn-
meal assemble near at hand.   A priest draws with the sacred
meal a circle on the ground.   Into this circle all the snakes
are hurled, forming a coil-
ing pyramid of horror.
For an instant the dancers
pause, and then on a signal
all rush forward, plunging
their arms into the writh-
ing heap, and seize as
many reptiles as the hand
will hold.   The little boy-
priest emerges from the
scramble with four snakes
longer than himself.   And
then away dash the fren-
zied bearers with their
garlands of intertangled
serpents, down the steep
trails toward the desert

Photograph by Sumner W. Matteson
SHOOTING THE " LIGHTNING FRAME "

Photograph by Sumner W. Matteson

THE FLUTE FRATERNITY AT A SPRING

Photograph by Sumner W. Matteson

MAKING THUNDER

which has grown dark and somber, for the sun has set. Far
and wide the priests have scattered, lost in the dimness of

Photograph by Sumner W. Matteson

A FEAST FOR THE FASTERS

the world below. When half an hour later they return, their
hands are empty, the snakes, messengers sure of a hearing with
the spirits of the underworld, have been set at liberty and are
now bearing the petitions of the people to the rulers of the rains.

The Snake Men strip and bathe at the spring below, enter
their kiva, deposit their ceremonial trappings, and finally in
simple scant attire they gather on the roof of the kiva and
drink huge bowls of nauseous emetic, enduring with stoical

Photograph by H. C. Vroman, Pasadena

PURIFICATION!

unconcern the inevitable, immediate result. This "ceremony of purification" ended, a feast begins, and the succeeding days are spent in revelry. No accidents have marked
the celebration, apparently so perilous. No dancers have
been bitten by the snakes.

At past performances, however, trustworthy witnesses
have seen the rattlesnakes draw blood from Moki arms, but
never has a death resulted from the bite. Scientific observ-
ers have captured rattlers after their release by the priests,

and on examination the fangs were found intact, the poison-
sacs well filled with deadly venom. We do not know why
the holy men of Moki Land do not fear the rattlesnake nor
how they render its dreaded fangs innocuous. We hear
vague rumors of a magical concoction, a broth brewed from
the juice of beetles — an antidote more efficacious than the
familiar " bug juice " employed by the white man in similar

Photograph by Sumner W. Matteson   A FLUTE CEREMONY AT A SPRING

emergencies. But of this we have no certain knowledge.
The secret of immunity remains a Hopi secret, jealously
guarded by the successive generations of the brotherhoods.

The Snake Dance closes with a glorious sunset built up
by the dark clouds which have assembled to witness all those
strange rites which every year are celebrated in their honor.
And it is an incontrovertible fact that Hopi prayers are
usually far more efficacious in bringing rains than are the

prayers of the average country clergymen. It may be that the cunning priests know from experience when the rains may be expected, and time their ceremonies accordingly. Still, that is no slight achievement, for the date of the Snake Dance is announced nineteen days in advance.

The line of the desert horizon seen from the Hopi villages is broken by a series of buttes and mesas sharply outlined against the sky. The Hopi priests regard that circle of shapes as the zodiac in their annual calculations. When

Photograph by Sumner W. Matteson, Sept. 15, 1901

THE ORAIBI FLUTE ALTAR

EVERYTHING INDICATES COMING RAIN — DUCKS COMING OUT — SWALLOWS FLYING
HOME — LIGHTNINGS — BLOSSOMING EARTH — LINES OF FALLING RAIN

LALLACONTE CEREMONY AT WALPI, SEPT. 5, 1901

the sun rises or sets behind a
certain butte or at the
edge of a certain
mesa, then the
observance of a
certain rite is
imperative.
The day fol-
lowing the in-
vocation held
at Oraibi in 1898
there burst over
the villages a terrific
thunder-storm.   In the
north heavens were as black
as night, fierce lightnings flashed, and
the rain descended, as if entire lakes had been snatched up

THE RAIN GODS
HEAR AND RESPOND

A WORLD-WIDE PASTURE

by the grateful Rain Gods, wrapped in black vapors, and dis-
patched to Moki Land in answer to the prayers of the Good
People.   Yet the downpour fell only upon the Moki mesas

Photograph by Sumner W. Matteson   MOKI GOATS

and upon tne Moki fields. We were then several miles away, en route to the railway; no rain fell where we stood, halting in silent wonder at the spectacle, for while the north sky was hidden by that black curtain of the storm, the south sky, toward which we were re- treating, was ar- tistically draped with lace-like clouds upon a background of pale blue.

Red mesas, a day's journey distant, seemed in the clear sharp atmosphere within a few miles of our path. Here and there we came upon a flock of sheep or goats belonging to the Navajos, for "Lo, the poor Indian" is not poor in Ari- zona. The Navajo nation is immensely rich in cat- tle, sheep, and horses. The tribe possesses one million six hun- dred thousand sheep, sixty thousand head of cattle, three hun- dred thousand goats, and so many horses that no equine census exists.

A NAVAJO BAMBINO

At Volz's Emporium No. 2, at The Lakes, we find a multitude of Navajos assembled.   The trader is about to give his annual "treat" to his customers.   He has announced a two-day tournament, offered prizes for contests and races,

A NAVAJO ROUND-UP AT THE LAKES

and invited the entire blue-book list of Navajo Land, agreeing to feed the braves, their wives, and children, for two days.   When we arrive, the guests are already gathered.   They come from far and near ; some families have ridden a hundred and fifty miles to attend the grandest social function of the year.   The men bring rifles and lariats, the women blankets and papooses.   We make a rough count of the visitors. There are about four hundred of them, a Navajo "four hundred" representing the best blood

21

EARLY ARRIVALS

and the greatest wealth of an old, heroic, wealthy tribe.
These people are far more hardy than the Mokis, more admir-
able in many ways, but far less civilized. The trader arranges
with the chiefs the details of the ceremonies and the contests.
First there will be a grand march, led by Mr. Volz, the host,
and the old Chief, whom all the guests treat with much respect.
Then a pony race with Navajo boys as jockeys, then a foot-
race contested by both Mokis and Navajos, and one American college man. The latter has the advantage at the start,
but when the runners cross a stretch of loose sand, he falls
behind. The barefoot Indians skim over the soft places.
A Moki wins. The colors of Cornell do not get even a place,
the white man being the fourth to cross the line.

THE ROOSTER-PLUCKING CONTEST

Photograph by H. C. Vroman, Pasadena

"RATTLESNAKE JACK"

Then comes the *Gallo* race or rooster - plucking contest, one of the most exciting sports of the big southwest.

A live rooster is buried in the sand, with its protesting head left protruding like a curious animated plant.

Photograph by Sumner W. Matteson

A NAVAJO SILVERSMITH

Many savage cavaliers assemble in the distance and one by one they ride furiously toward us. Then, as they near the red comb of the gallo, they gracefully swing earthward from the saddle, making a swift grab at the protruding neck in an endeavor to jerk the rooster from the sand and thus secure the prize. The feat is difficult, and of the forty or fifty riders only a few even touch the wriggling bait. Innumerable grabs are made, sandy clouds are raised, horses stumble, the horsemen almost lose their

Photograph by Sumner W. Matteson

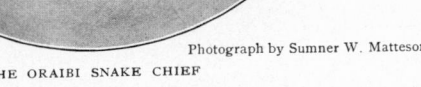

THE ORAIBI SNAKE CHIEF

balance, and still the cock remains untouched.   But at last
the screaming bird is gripped by some skilful hand and deftly
disinterred.   Then away dashes the successful brave, followed
by a squadron of desperate red men, each one intent on secur-
ing a wing or leg of that unhappy fowl.   Ten minutes later the
prize has been torn into a hundred shreds and every bloody-
handed Navajo possesses some gory souvenir of the struggle.

Photograph by H. C. Vroman, Pasadena

A NAVAJO HOGAN

Among the spectators not one is more enthusiastic than
"Rattlesnake Jack," the bravest and most daring member of
our caravan.   "Jack" was a girl from Denver.   We called
her "Jack" because she liked the name, and used the pre-
fix, "Rattlesnake," because she carried in her pocket a
beautiful collection of rattles which she had calmly cut with
a penknife from protesting rattlers' tails.   There is many a

RATTLESNAKE JACK PURSUED BY A BAND OF NAVAJOS

dumb snake wandering unhappily in the great desert, thanks to the campaign waged by Rattlesnake Jack.

Jack is the heroine of one of the most thrilling motion-pictures made in Arizona. She is determined to experience the sensations of one pursued by a band of Indians. She challenges the braves to catch her, mounts the chief's horse, and dashes away, followed by a mob of mounted savages.

"AMONG THOSE PRESENT"

They fail to overtake her, and after the race, obediently follow her, ranging themselves before the camera as she rides forward and salutes the spectators.

The Navajos are lost in admiration for the daughter of the pale-face, and her exploits will long be talked of in the crude desert dwellings or "hogans" of the tribe. The tournament of '98 will be memorable among them because of her; but that of '99 will be more memorable,

because in that year the Indians beheld a miracle.   The
same white men come again, one year later, bringing strange
instruments and a big white sheet, which they stretch on the
outer wall of Volz's store.   Then, after night has fallen, half
a thousand red men, crouching in the sand, behold upon that
white surface huge pictures in which men seem to live and

THE GUESTS OF TRADER VOLZ

move.   They view the moving multitudes in the streets of
far-off cities ; they *see* the railway trains that they have
merely heard about ; they see themselves performing deeds
which they know were performed twelve months before.
But what astounds them most is the appearance in life upon
that screen of tribesmen who have died during the intervening

DAUGHTERS OF THE DESERT

year, or others whom they know are far away. As each familiar figure passes, the dumbfounded spectators start to utter cries of consternation, then clap their hands over their mouths and try to smother the incipient yells, so that the ghosts shall not become frightened and disappear. Strange to relate, no curiosity at all

AT THE RACES

is excited by the projecting instrument, but the canvas screen is minutely examined by the nonplused Navajos who finger it and rub their cheeks against it, as if to detect some sign of life or of sorcery in the white fabric.

After the tournament is ended, feasting begins; then, late at night, shadowy forms assemble near the store and perform weird dances. A hundred Navajos in a circle, elbow to elbow, move slowly round and round, with a stamping step, chanting strange songs. We, too, take places in the ring and become almost hypnotized by the rhythm and the movement and the ruddy glare of the fire around which we are circling. All night the dancers sing and circle; when we are roused just before sunrise, to prepare for departure, wild monotonous chanting still comes to us from distant

BEDOUINS OF THE SOUTHWEST

RATTLESNAKE JACK AFTER THE RACE

"hogans," where at least a remnant of the tireless braves
are persisting in their somber all-night revel.

We ride away while the desert is still hid in the purple
shadows, for we have nearly thirty miles to cover in the next
four hours, else we shall miss the eastbound express. We
are not eager to return to civilization ; the charm of the

BACK TOWARD THE WORLD OF CITIES

desert is still upon us ; we have not yet drunk deep enough
of its life-giving air ; we have not yet satisfied our eyes with
looking at the wide horizon. The Painted Desert, stretching
away toward the Grand Cañon, spreads out a tempting feast
of space and color. The Painted Desert is the most alluring
desert in the world ; a gorgeous expanse of tinted sands and
rocks and ledges painted by Nature when the earth was young.

But there is no water there, and we dare not venture
westward toward that realm of beauty, thirst, and death.

Therefore we set our faces toward the south, toward the railway and the world of cities ; and as we ride, the magic colors fade away from earth and sky, save for a faint tinge of yellow that lingers overhead, a last reflection of the sandy world which we are leaving with regret.

The fascination of the desert, the charm of the *flat places* of the earth cannot be explained. It must be felt. If you would know one of the most wholesome joys of life, go buy a saddle and a bridle, a bronco, and a blanket, and forgetting all the petty things of life ride away into this Sahara of our glorious southwest, and there find the true meaning of such words as space — exhilaration — freedom !